CONFESSIONS OF A SERIAL ALIBI

Asia McClain Chapman

A POST HILL PRESS BOOK
ISBN: 978-1-68261-158-6
ISBN (eBook): 978-1-68261-159-3

CONFESSIONS OF A SERIAL ALIBI
© 2016 by Asia McClain Chapman
All Rights Reserved

Cover Design by Quincy Alivio
Cover Photograph by Danielle Castilla

Post Hill Press
275 Madison Avenue, 14th Floor
New York, NY 10016
posthillpress.com

To my children
Mommy loves you.

CONTENTS

PREFACE

My lawyer Gary Proctor says it's better to not add fuel to the fire; however, after over a year of feeling swallowed by the enigma that has been the SERIAL podcast, I feel my sensibilities starting to slip. I operate under the understanding that I must silence my opinions for the sake of my own integrity. However, not defending myself publicly has started to eat away at my strong sense of self-confidence. From the moment I first heard the SERIAL podcast, I started to feel a heavier weight on my shoulders. After listening to the podcast I came to understand that I had made a grave mistake. I had put my trust in the wrong hands and that justice may have taken a back seat to naiveté. I soon desperately struggled to make sense of everything that had happened behind my back. Like many of my fellow SERIAL followers there was no sense to be made, no clarity to be given. There was no smoking gun or red gloves, as it were. What there was, however, was a lot of gossip and numerous speculations. The more I learned, the more uncertain I became about who killed Hae. Being a person who values the truth, character and integrity, one thing did become abundantly clear to me: my character and motivations were under fire and up for public scrutiny.

As much as I tried to tune it out, SERIAL and its media coverage was staring me in the face every time I scrolled through my Facebook newsfeed, typed my name into Google or watched the news. I couldn't even watch the Times Square New Year's Eve special without mention made to it. It seemed as if the more the case evolved, the more the infamy began to stress me out. Mainly because, as Gary said, it was in my best interest to say nothing and let my affidavits speak for themselves. In theory that's stellar advice, however in reality and in practice it's a bitter pill to swallow. In doing so, I began to feel anxiety creeping in, feelings that I had worked so hard to eliminate many moons ago when faced with a traumatic bout of workplace racial discrimination. Sometimes I didn't sleep much but when I did sleep, I would have twisted nightmares. I admit, I would often cry over the intense responsibility I felt, as well as the scrutiny placed on my character and intelligence. I started becoming hyper-sensitive to the slightest criticisms. I began to get pretty edgy with everyone in my life, including my own young children.

On a whim I started writing in order to relieve some of my tension, to say the things that I wasn't able to say online or to the press. However, again, even in my journal, it seemed as if my thoughts were useless because no one was aware of them. Then one day a friend said, "You should write a book!" and it dawned on me: I can say something to the public, just not now. There were things I so desperately wanted to address but had been advised against for obvious timing reasons. That night, I began typing on my laptop. I was at it for two hours straight and had probably filled three quarters of a full legal pad with notes. That was when I knew I had to write this book. There was so much that needed to be addressed that my concerns seemed endless. Sometimes it became exhausting to think of all the questions and comments that people were making, things they wanted to know and ask me. By the way, this process has been very overwhelming at times. The memory recall involved has been extremely draining. The openness required has been emotionally taxing and something that I have had great reservations about. By the sheer nature of this situation, there is a great level of expectation and attention placed on me. Being thrust into the public limelight has been quite stressful at times. Some days it's harder to accept than others. Some days I'm okay with it and some days I just want to bury my head in the sand. From the very beginning I told Adnan I hoped he appreciated me coming forward, because I would "really rather not be a part of this." I still feel the same way but more so in terms of our criminal justice system. This experience hasn't been easy and I hope that everyone can appreciate my commitment to doing the right thing. As people often point out, Adnan could be any one of us. Keeping that in mind as I'm writing this, I can only say that there are three main reasons that I am writing this book.

My first and foremost reason for writing this book is for my children. When they're old enough, I want them to know what happened. I want them to know why their mom made the mistakes that she made. I want them to understand what was done in an attempt to correct those mistakes and that their mom was tough, that I stood firm and did the right thing even when it was difficult. I want to impose upon them a legacy of integrity and let them know that telling the truth is important.

Secondly, I'm writing this book for myself and my own sanity. The hardest thing about this whole ordeal is the isolation. Right now I'm trying my damndest to do the right thing by making myself accessible to both sides of the court, all the while without making myself too accessible to the misleading eye of the media. I've already had a hard and fast lesson on who not to trust. This time around I'm super careful about who I trust and who I speak to. I've already seen how my words can be misunderstood, twisted, changed or over-examined like they're under a microscope. Having that already happen to me over and over again has made me especially guarded when it comes to my opinions about this case. As you can imagine, there aren't a lot of people that I can talk to about this stuff, outside of my husband and my lawyer, Gary Proctor. Anyone else that I have conversations with can run to social and traditional media outlets with statements. They could potentially "Urick me" (as they say online) with misrepresentations and I'm not about to have that happen again. I'm writing this book as a form of self-therapy. Social media is a ruthless place to air one's grievances. It's too fast-paced, too easily misquoted and it's too easily lost in the vacuum of the Internet. A book seemed more conclusive and final. It's a frustrating thing to have people all over the world questioning me and I can't address things in one concise spot. My lawyer told me the Friday before my new affidavit was released that I had to "get it out," because I was "literally about to burst." So this is my way of getting "it" all out. I'm going to try my best to address questions, speculations and comments and get this whole experience off my chest. In fact, since I started writing, my stress level has lowered so much and I've been able to think more clearly. When it's all said and done, I will have hopefully said all there really is to say. That idea alone is one that is very comforting to me.

The third reason that I am writing this book is for all of you #Serial, #FreeAdnan, #AdnanSyed, #JusticeforHae and #AsiaMcClain enthusiasts. I want you to remember that all of us involved in this tragic event are real people, not characters. I can't speak for the evaluations about others, but some of you have been spot on in your Asia McClain theories. The remainder of you could not be further from the truth with your speculations. Some of your accusations are as baseless as they are rational. Many of you have issued me kind words of support (that have been greatly appreciated). To those of you who have shared kind words, I want to say thank you. To those of you with overactive imaginations and insulting insinuations, I'd like to set you straight. Or at least try. I'll start off by saying that I'm not a liar, a pushover, I'm not a fool and nobody is going to bully me. I am, or rather, I was, Asia McClain, and this is my story.

LIFE IN 1999

Media attention in a criminal case like Adnan Syed's is seldom very notable. Now, normally, a conviction of this magnitude would not only be considered run of the mill. It would probably be deemed easily solvable. For example, there's seventeen-year-old Hae Min Lee, a beautiful young Asian girl. A girl whom someone kidnaps and possibly holds against her will before finally murdering her in the prime of her promising life. Adnan Syed, her allegedly possessive, sadistic, jealous ex-boyfriend who stands convicted of her murder. Jay Wilds, the apprehensive and sketchy accomplice who not only testifies to assisting with the burial of Hae's body, but also helps to corroborate the state prosecutor's narrative in exchange for a plea deal. Slam dunk for the state's upcoming, eager prosecutor Kevin Urick, right? Well…not quite.

See, in this cluster of a murder case, things have failed to be that simple. In this case Jay Wilds has pathologically changed his story multiple times, proving himself to be an extremely unreliable state's witness. Adnan is the antithesis of the jealous ex-lover, and after sixteen years has maintained that he neither has knowledge, motive nor any involvement in the murder of his beloved friend and ex-girlfriend. Then there's Hae Min Lee, a strong, athletic and smart girl strangled to death by one or many sick predators that day. Nonetheless there is not a single piece of evidence that undeniably points to how, when or where the crime took place and who did it. All the while, for more than a decade Adnan Syed has been remanded in prison while his accomplice Jay Wilds has gotten off scot free with nothing more than a slap on the wrist. Then there is the State of Maryland's prosecutor Kevin Urick, a man who by all other accounts was able to ride off into the sunset, as the hero on the side of justice. A man who by all accounts used his silver-lined tongue to sweet talk his fallacious evidence to both the jury and key witnesses. Then there's myself of course. Asia McClain, the wide-eyed teenage girl who over the course of sixteen years has become an avid community leader and stay-at-home mother of two. Known among few circles as Adnan's key alibi witness for the time of the murder but was never contacted by the defense attorney. A person who by all intents and purposes slipped through the cracks of the criminal justice system.

Yep, that's pretty much how the court and history itself had recorded things as of 2010. That was until four years later, when Sarah Koenig arrived on the scene. Sarah Koenig was introduced to Adnan's case by a close family friend of Adnan's, Rabia Chaudry. Rabia's younger brother Saad was best friends with Adnan and Rabia had a strong familiarization with the evidence presented at the time of Adnan's trial. Concerned about some of the ethics and procedures that took place within the police investigation and trial itself, Rabia reached out to Sarah Koenig. Sarah responded by breathing new life into Adnan's story. Sarah began to investigate claims both disclosed and undisclosed at trial and as a result, she uncovered never before publicized testimonies from previously unknown and/or unreachable witnesses. Sarah conducted real time simulations of the state's theorized time of murder, she combed through cell phone tower records, conducted interviews and she asked important questions that no one in the media had ever asked about Syed's trial and post-conviction hearing. As a testament to her creativity and resourcefulness, she spoke to experts in both the fields of psychology and law, all of which commanded the attention of millions of listeners, one of which was myself, Asia McClain. Now if you don't know already, this is the story of my involvement in the case of the State of Maryland vs. Adnan Syed. This is my perspective of a case and story that you probably have come to refer to as SERIAL.

Woodlawn High School was like one of those schools that

you see in movies like *The Substitute*. Although there were many exceptional and well-behaved students that bloomed from the school, Woodlawn certainly had its fair share of thugs and delinquent students. The student body population was full of amateur drug dealers, users and all around troublemakers. Upon recently chatting with my best friends, I discovered that many of them could recall sentiments of parental displeasure when they expressed interest in attending the school after junior high. Woodlawn's only saving grace for my generation was a zero tolerance principal who was set to take over our freshman year. Despite Dr. Wilson's no nonsense zero tolerance policies, there were still fights at the school just about every day. A lot of the fights were pretty violent and involved people being seriously injured. I can remember instances of stabbings, people getting thrown through windows and display cases. Group beat downs and neighborhood gang fights were something that we were all very familiar with. I can remember attending sporting events in which Woodlawn students would fight rival Milford Mill and Randallstown High School students as if we lived within the pages of *West Side Story*. I remember one incident in particular, in which the Baltimore County Police ended up pepper spraying a varsity basketball game. I believe video from that incident is still available on YouTube to this day. There were students sneaking marijuana in every crevice of the school corridors. One time someone almost accidently set the school on fire while sneaking a smoke in the boy's locker room. Teenage sex ran rapid in the downstairs band wing, on the catwalk and backstage and in other dark areas of the school's auditorium. I myself wasn't privy to any of those activities, but I did have my own share of other teenage shenanigans.

As far as the SERIAL story is concerned, the problems with Hae and Adnan's relationship started at Woodlawn High School, in the year 1999. However, if you ask some of our fellow classmates and I, we'd all tell you that this story started long before around the time shortly after our eleventh grade junior prom. For most, this event signaled the beginning of Hae and Adnan's relationship, because they attended the dance together and thereafter began dating. On the outside they were a truly adorable couple—a prime example of our country's ever-growing interracial couple population. They were both excellent students, well-liked and accomplished school athletes. Although I didn't know either intimately, we all shared the same friends and crossed paths many a time, so I can speak to the caliber of students that they were. To anyone outside of our friendship circle, there probably wasn't much (if any) indication of trouble within their relationship. The only time that I can remember things getting truly out of hand was when Adnan's parents found out that he had taken a girl (Hae) to our senior homecoming dance. As a result, Adnan's parents decided it was best to show up at the event and make a huge scene, leaving both parties mortified.

That in itself was the catalyst of their doomed relationship, ironically very similar to Romeo and Juliet. Their parents
were the problem in their relationship. In my opinion, had their
parents' disapproval not been a factor, things may have ended
up much differently for those two. I certainly don't say that to
blame their parents, rather just to say that the discourse was a
negative factor in the teens' relationship. I acknowledge that had
things been different, it remains to be seen whether Hae might
still be alive. We don't 100 percent know who killed her, but I
do think Adnan would have been less likely to have been her
ex-boyfriend at the time of her murder and as a result, may have
been painted in a different light (if painted at all). The reason
that I make such a bold statement is because in an attempt to
pander to their parents, Hae and Adnan were ultimately forced
to repress their relationship from their families. For fear of what
I like to call "parental repercussions" they had to hide one another's existence. When my fellow classmates and I were flourishing
in the art of introducing our significant others to our families,
Hae and Adnan lived that part of their lives in secrecy. Having
a relationship littered with secret hookups and strategically
planned phone calls placed a heavy burden on their otherwise
jovial relationship. Although they cared deeply and loved one
another, they weren't entirely free to express it and as a result
it made things more complicated, stressful and ultimately less
ideal for Hae in particular.

So there we were, us three, all seniors at Woodlawn High School, preparing ourselves for graduation into "the real world." All completely unaware of how much our brief encounters with one another would actually matter in the years to come. Back then, we were all so happy and full of promise and options. I don't think any of us could have truly conceived how our lives would have turned out. I don't think anyone can, at that age. I often laugh when I think about the many ideas that I used to have about my future. One in particular was the idea that I wanted to be a criminal psychologist for the FBI. I don't even think that was ever true. I do recall having an interest in psychology when I first graduated from high school. All my life I've been a natural empath, able to strongly sense the feelings of others. At the time I thought psychology would be a good fit for me, giving me the chance to help society and make a difference. I did take a few psychology classes in college, however I had no real idea of what I wanted my career to be, at that point in my life. I thought psychology seemed like a good field of study in order to achieve my lifestyle desires, but then I found out about all the necessary requirements needed in order to have a private practice. Since I had been raised in a household of mostly government employees, for a brief time I bargained that using psychology in conjunction with a government agency (FBI) might be the better way to go. After all, entry-level positions require less school and tend to pay better initially. Eventually I lost interest in pursuing psychology all together because I found the stress of other people's psychological struggles to be too much for me to healthily process. In a different yet somewhat comical light, I also recall wanting to become a veterinarian at one point. At least until I found out about expressing anal glands, animal cancers and euthanasia.

I guess now is as good as any time to start setting the record straight. I sometimes have a problem with the word "friends." Sometimes, I refer to people as friends who are mere acquaintances. Never really thought about it as a problem until this case. I suppose one does not truly consider many things about oneself until being examined by millions of people all over the world. Simply put, I wasn't an especially close friend of Hae and Adnan's. We weren't truly friends at all. The three of us were friendly towards one another and we did speak on occasion, but that was it. Adnan was friends with many of my high school buddies at the time of our senior year. One of my closest friends to this day was Adnan's football captain back in our senior year of high school. My good friend and tenth grade ex-boyfriend Justin was a close friend of Adnan's before all this happened. To put things into perspective, Justin and Adnan lived in the same neighborhood and had many of the same friends. Justin's family was very close to Stephanie's (Jay's girlfriend) family, and Stephanie was very close to Adnan. Similar to Adnan, Hae was friends with a number of my high school friends. Both Hae and I were fairly popular in high school, as were most athletes, therefore many of our various teammates were often the same people. In addition, over the four years that I had spent at Woodlawn, I had several brief encounters with Hae and Adnan alike. Now let me just say this: from what I knew about Hae Min Lee, she was no wimp. She was headstrong but gracious when she needed to be. By many accounts, Woodlawn High School was pretty rough and Hae's ability to flourish within the student body population was not by happenstance. Although she was from an immigrant family, Hae was very Americanized. She had plenty of people she called friends and a healthy teenage social life. From what I recall Hae was also a pretty resilient athlete, playing both girls' field hockey and lacrosse. By no means was she weak, easily manipulated, bullied or unconfident about herself.

Now I know female lacrosse and field hockey players (in particular) don't always get a tremendous amount of accolades in the realm of being total badasses, but let me tell you, they are! I tried out once for both sports and although I was an established athlete in my own right I couldn't cut it. For one, I had childhood asthma and try as I did, I just didn't have the stamina for all the non-stop running during practices. I can recall many a practice where players were required to run the circumference of the school property. During those practices I thought my heart was going to literally leap right out of my chest. My leg muscles felt like they were going to burst and my lunch "came up" (for a lack of better words). The other reason that I decided that lacrosse wasn't for me was because I found myself not able to shake the fear of being seriously hurt or accidentally hurting other players. I remember one lacrosse game in particular where I had attempted to "check" an opponent and accidentally "checked" her in the nose. For all you people that don't follow lacrosse that means my lacrosse stick ended up cracking the poor girl right in her face. Although it was an accident, I was immediately red flagged by the referee and pulled out of the game by the coach. In that moment, I found myself both benched and subsequently somewhat traumatized by the fact that I had harmed someone so intensely. Meanwhile the poor girl that I had hit was dealing with a bloody and most likely broken nose. The rest of the game is a blur to me and soon after I quit the team. To this day, I just can't imagine a scenario in which an athlete like Hae (with that kind of endurance and fearlessness) didn't fight for her life. In my opinion there had to have been two assailants or some circumstances that impaired her greatly in order for her to have been strangled to death. Perhaps someone held her down while another person choked her. Or perhaps there was only one assailant and that person simply choked her while she was already unconscious. Lord knows, that's the only way I would have gone out. Even us Baltimore County kids are *still* Baltimore kids. We know how to protect ourselves. We're pretty scrappy, if I say so myself.

On a brighter note, I was the girl who was cool with everybody in high school. Didn't matter if you were a self-proclaimed beauty queen, a jock or of the slightly nerdier variety, I knew and was friends with just about everyone at Woodlawn. As my friends back then and now could tell you, I was a "social butterfly." I even vaguely remember being nominated for one of our school dance positions, I believe it was prom queen (I made reference to it in my senior book). Winning such things wasn't especially important to me so I told my supporters to send their votes to my friends. Needless to say, the fact that Adnan and I held a conversation in the library on January of 1999 is not odd in the slightest. It doesn't strike anyone who knew either one of us as out of place either. The fact that I asked him about his breakup with Hae wasn't awkward at all. We had a lot of the same friends and it was common knowledge within our social circle. Now let this be said: me asking Adnan about his breakup wasn't an attempt at flirting with him nor was it information that Adnan randomly volunteered to me. In fact, I was the one who brought it up to him. In my defense, I literally could not think of anything else to ask him at that particular moment. Looking back, perhaps I should have led with a different topic, but I digress. I had been at the Woodlawn Public library for so long that day that I was dying to talk to someone.

Back in January of 1999, I was enrolled in my school's co-operative education program for students that had fulfilled all of their required graduation credit hours. I was permitted to leave the school grounds every day at 10:40 AM, in order to get more hours at my part-time job. Every day, I would attend a couple of morning classes and then usually report to the "co-op teacher" (Mrs. Graham?) at the start of third period. Once there, I'd check out of school and wait to be dismissed for the day. When I began the program, I had held a job as a cashier at Dunkin' Donuts on Liberty Road. However, by this time in the school year I was no longer working at the donut shop. Fortunately for me, Woodlawn High School was not very good about verifying our employment after enrollment into the co-op program. Plus, I had conveniently failed to report this change to the school. So instead of going to my employer's location, I would take the yellow co-op school bus to another student's work location closest to my house. I would then walk whatever remaining distance back to my house. This was not always favorable because sometimes the nearest work location was a great distance from my home. So after some thought I began having my then-boyfriend Derrick come pick me up at the Woodlawn campus and he would take me wherever I wanted to go (usually his house or my home). Coincidentally, a short time after Hae was found dead, Derrick conceded to loaning me his car in the early mornings. That arrangement made it unnecessary for me to have to wait on him anymore. Usually, my best friend Marie drove her mother's cargo van to school, so I'd have her drop me off at Derrick's house in the mornings. I would then snag Derrick's vehicle, go to school at Woodlawn and then have it back to Derrick by the time school was out at Milford Mill High School. Derrick lived across the street from Milford Mill back in 1999. Technically Derrick didn't need a car to get to school; he merely drove it there and parked it in the student parking lot for "coolness points." Now I can't recall 100 percent if our final car arrangement was related to the fight we had on the day of Hae's disappearance (him being late and me being tired of having to wait on him for a ride) or if it was related specifically to Hae's disappearance or death (fearing for my safety). I do know that its general purpose was to make things less complicated and safe for me. By any account, at the time Hae went missing I was not using Derrick's car on my own yet and Derrick didn't usually pick me up from the public library. That particular day, I walked across the campus to the Woodlawn Public Library in order to await Derrick's arrival. When Derrick didn't show up during his scheduled lunch hour, I became concerned. When he hadn't showed up several hours later, my concern changed into annoyance, then anger and ultimately boredom. Being that I had been stranded alone in the public library for over four hours, I was extremely bored and probably would have talked to anyone that I knew about anything. Regrettably, because of the nature of high school gossip, Hae and Adnan's breakup was fresh on my mind. As such, that's what came out first when my conversation with Adnan transpired. Had Derrick not shown up when he did, my conversation with Adnan probably would have segued into other topics outside of the breakup. It's just that it never got the chance, because Derrick and Jerrod arrived when they did. As I think about my first description of that conversation with Adnan, I smirk because the first time that I told Justin about it and described Adnan's sentiments about the break up I believed I used a phrase similar to "there's other fish in the sea kind of attitude." Consequently, that's now a little ironic that I made such a statement. I now know (from the podcast) that Adnan was already dating other girls by that point in high school. So long story short, I wasn't some random nobody asking highly personal questions to Adnan, I was a familiar face within his already existing social circle. The only disconnect if any, can be contributed to what Jay Wilds said about the magnet program in part one of his Intercept interview:

"When Woodlawn put in the magnet thing, they took out all the vocational classes. Before you would just go down there for drafting, shop, and everyone would co-mingle, and all the students interacted. But when they put the magnet wing in, it was kind of like these people were different from us. And they didn't have to interact with us anymore. They didn't have to go by except to come to lunch, and that was it. But their gym, lockers, parking, was down in the magnet wing."

All my best friends back in high school were all "magnet kids" along with Hae and Adnan. I usually only saw my best friends at lunch, after school for sports, at special events or afterwards around town. My husband likes to tease me about it, but in all truth I was a sort of honorary "magnet kid." For this reason, it was quite common for one of my "magnet friends" to tie me to another person (whether magnet or not) in some way. Adnan and Hae were just two of those "friend's friends" that I hadn't gotten to know on a personal level yet.

Ask anyone who has listened to SERIAL and they will tell you that the subject of memory reliability is one of the underlying repetitive themes within the podcast. In the beginning of the twelve-episode series, Sarah Koenig addresses the slippery nature of memory as it applies to everyone involved in the Syed case. Sarah then continues by giving examples of questionable memories through her discovery of the various testimonies given both inside and outside of the Syed trial. Adnan, Jay and myself are of particular interest; however, there are other players such as Inez, Summer, Krista and Jenn. Many people have asked how is it that I can remember January 13th, 1999 so well. I have often asked myself the same question. There are several reasons that the events of January 13th stand out in my memory. The most personal is that I was in love with Derrick at the time and when love disappoints you, it's remembered. Being left stranded at the public library that day was the first of many embarrassing disappointments from Derrick. I don't say that to be mean or scornful, but to simply be honest. Derrick was my first love and he ultimately was the first to break my heart. As they say, "Hindsight is twenty-twenty," so at the time, I could not see all that he was doing behind my back. Nor could I see that he was not a very good boyfriend. During the relationship we had constant ups and downs. There would be times when things would be wonderful and times when things were on the verge of ending between us. Our relationship lasted three years and it was plagued with drama and high emotions, as it goes in most teenage relationships, I suppose.

So what is memory? Webster's online dictionary defines memory as "the faculty of the mind by which it retains the knowledge of previous thoughts, impressions, or events. Memory is the purveyor of reason."

If that is true, then that should also bring into question the nature of false memories and lack of memory as well. We already know that people are often capable of misremembering previously conceptualized thoughts, impressions and events. We know this because of conditions like amnesia and false memory syndrome. For myself, I know that seeing Adnan in the library on January 13th happened on that specific day because I know what living with false and implanted memories feels like. Memory itself is a sore subject with me and has been a constant source of distress and sorrow within my personal life. Although I don't talk about it often, I am quite troubled by the absence of many early important memories. This stands to explain (to me) why I hold such certainty about other memories like my conversation with Adnan.

I was born in June of 1981 in Inglewood, California. A few years before I was born my mother traveled to the city to stay with her favorite aunt and cousin. Soon after she ended up meeting and falling in love with my father, a California native. Within no time, they were married at a courthouse and within months, I was conceived. At first things were wonderful between my parents; they were young and full of tenacity. Never mind that they were both often working ten- and twelve-hour shifts at work. They had me and each other and that was what made them happy. Unfortunately, like most young and under-established relationships, they grew apart and as a result, they separated when I was about five years old. Now I couldn't tell you to what degree of marital discourse they experienced, because unfortunately I have no memory of my toddler years at all. In fact, I don't have any genuine memories of my life prior to my ninth birthday party. I use the term genuine because there are a few things that I do recall about my early years. Sadly, I'm not even sure whether many of them are false or implanted memories because they are heavily associated with family stories and home videos that I've seen a hundred times. I've recently started some spiritual counseling with the hopes of recovering real memories. It's a slow process but I hope that in time I will recover something. I've even more recently opened myself to the idea of hypnotherapy. Nonetheless the reason my ninth birthday party sticks out as my first real memory is because that is the first time I can recall details of my own accord. At the time I was in love with New Kids on the Block, so much so that they were the central theme of my party. I had New Kids decorations, New Kids posters and even a New Kids themed birthday cake design. In addition to all the fanfare my ninth birthday party was also my first sleepover. All my closest friends crowded together in sleeping bags in my grandparents' basement, watched cable television, goofed off and had hours of girl talk and mischief. Speaking of which, my younger cousin India was encouraged to "surf" the arm of my grandparents' rocking chair (like the rest of us had already done) and as a result, she slipped and split her temple open. She ended up having to leave to get stitches and she still has a small scar to this day (sorry, cuz). That's how most of my memories are preserved—they are tied to significant events or emotions. I don't know what led me to start blocking out my memories as a child. Whatever it was, it was traumatic enough to make me develop a form of protective amnesia. A few years back, I read an article on psychogenic amnesia and found it very interesting. For those of you who aren't familiar with the term, human-memory.net defines psychogenic amnesia as follows:

"Psychogenic amnesia, also known as functional amnesia or dissociative amnesia, is a disorder characterized by abnormal memory functioning in the absence of structural brain damage or a known neurobiological cause. It results from the effects of severe stress or psychological trauma on the brain, rather than from any physical or physiological cause. It is often considered to be equivalent to the clinical condition known as repressed memory syndrome."

Although that's very similar to what I feel happened to me as a child, I have yet to determine the source of said mental trauma. By all accounts I was never physically harmed, abused or molested, so there should be no problem, right? If you were to ask my husband, he would tell you that my memories are all or nothing. Either it's that I have a detailed memory that is tied to an event or emotion (that I remember forever), or chances are there is a limited or no memory at all. Don't get me wrong, I don't have Alzheimer's-type memory losses. I'm just like most people in the sense that I am quicker to forget details of certain events if I don't find them to be personally significant. For instance, I can tell you many details surrounding my first kiss but I have no idea what I ate for lunch last Tuesday. Now I don't know if the divorce of my parents and relocation across the United States (to Maryland) was enough to traumatize me that significantly. I don't know, perhaps it was and I was just sensitive? From what I have been told, my mother's and my return to Baltimore was not something that happened over night. It took a bit of financial planning and as a result I spent quite a bit of time with my grandparents and babysitters.

One thing that I do recall was the antics of a particular babysitter. I remember a few details as if it were yesterday. My babysitter was responsible for the daily care of an extremely elderly woman. I don't remember who the woman was in relation to my babysitter (maybe her mother?), I just remember that the woman was feeble-minded (probably had dementia) and bedridden. As I recall the woman did not speak at all and simply stared at a television screen all day. I know it's mean to say this, but I remember that the elderly woman scared me so much that my memories compare closely to that of Crypt Keeper. She had long thinning white hair, always wore a nightgown and usually sat upright in a hospital bed inside a small tight little room. I recall that I was given the duty of brushing this elderly woman's hair every day and that as a young kid, I hated it.

Another detail that I recall about my California babysitter is that she had a weird obsession with southern food, particularly black-eyed peas. I remember that she would serve them to me all the time, what seemed like every day. As you can imagine, I grew to hate the taste and smell of them, and after a while I began refusing to eat them. This of course only caused more of a problem, as my babysitter was not fond of me not eating her robust recipes. Consequently, to this day I still refuse to eat black-eyed peas or even be in the vicinity of either black-eyed peas or hospice facilities. I hate retirement homes and avoid them like the plague. So far I have been lucky enough to only visit a couple of elderly family members in hospice, so my exposure time has been limited.

So where does that leave me in terms of my memory of seeing Adnan where I did, when I did on January 13th, 1999? Absolutely clear. Ask anyone I know, when it comes to my memories, I am very clear on things that I can recall, things that I barely recall and things that I do not recall at all. When I say I remember something, I remember it and it indeed happened. Ironically during these types of discussions I am most often the only one who remembers a particular event and its details the best. I often am the one to jog my friends' memories about times long forgotten. That's why my friends often say I have the best memory in our group. In the same light, when I don't recall a particular event or its details, I am usually very clear about expressing that as well. If I'm unsure, I'll often use words such as "like," kind of," "sort of," and "maybe"—words that don't express certainty. Sometimes I can reconstruct unclear memories by talking myself through them in my mind. When I do this, I say I am "memory fishing," as I call it. I don't speak in absolutes and I will often communicate when I'm not certain about details. A prime example of this would be when I spoke to Sarah Koenig fourteen years after Adnan's conviction. During that interview, I attempted to recall the full extent of the type of the winter weather that transpired on January 13th, 1999. Needless to say, I tried on the fly and failed.

CHAPTER ONE

JANUARY 13TH, 1999

January 13th, 1999 started out purely normal. The plan for that day was for Derrick to come pick me up during his lunch hour, drop me off at his house and go back to school at Milford Mill High School. He obviously didn't stick to that plan, so I was left waiting in the library until after school let out at Woodlawn. As you can imagine this is also why I ended up getting so pissed at Derrick by the time he showed up. My early release school pass was for 10:40 AM. I left the school building shortly after that time. Derrick didn't arrive to pick me up until after 2:15 PM. All the school buses were already lined up in the school roundabout, waiting to take the majority of students off the school property. By the time Adnan showed up in the library, I was at the verge of being stranded (unless I got a ride from a friend back at the school, or caught public transportation, which I hated!). Understandably, I had been watching the library's main entrance like a hawk, hoping to see Derrick walk in. When that didn't happen, I was pretty happy to see Adnan's familiar face as a consolation prize. When I saw him in the library that day, he didn't seem to be flustered, nervous, preoccupied or suspicious in any way. In fact, he kind of just strolled in from what I remember. I actually saw him first and remember feeling relieved because the whole time I had been at the library, I hadn't seen anyone that I knew. Naturally I waved or smiled, probably both. He walked over to me, near the center of the library where the computers were located at that time. I remember that I was seated and had a book on the table in front of me but that I had only been looking at its pictures. It was an art history book, but I couldn't tell you the name of that book to save my life. Unfortunately I didn't check any materials out of the library that day (I've since checked), so that piece of information is also forever lost to me.

I didn't really know Adnan well, but he was very good friends with many of my best friends, including my ex-boyfriend Justin Adger. Years later I think a few individuals tried as hard as they could to make Adnan and I seem worlds apart but we really weren't. I'm sure Adnan knew all kinds of stuff about me, as far as Justin goes (i.e. our lack of a sex life, that I had a new boyfriend, etc.). Being that all my friends were "magnet kids" I had also heard a rumor that Hae and Adnan had recently broken up. I figured since Adnan had probably been privy to mine and Justin's "breakup story" I didn't think anything of asking him about the validity of his breakup rumor. In any case, there was a brief exchange of "what's ups" between us and then I said something to the effect of, "So I heard you and Hae broke up?" When I asked him this, I remember saying it with care because I didn't know how he'd respond. Sometimes high school guys try to act "harder" than they feel about breakups and sometimes people just don't want to talk about such things. Plus, I didn't know if it was a messy breakup or not so I didn't want to pry too hard, but I did want to know. I admit, after I said it, it did feel a little nosy to be asking, but to my surprise he simply said "Yeah" with a kind of disappointment in his tone. I'm not going to lie, this intrigued me, so I said something to the effect of "Dang, sorry, man" to show empathy.

Then that's when he said something like, "Noooo, it's all good. Me and her are good. I'm doing my thing and besides, she's seeing some other dude now, some white guy." Then he explained that he didn't have any hard feelings about anything and that ultimately he just wanted her to be happy. On a personal note, Adnan and Hae's post-breakup relationship was pretty similar to mine and Justin's the previous year. To me, there was nothing weird about Hae and Adnan still being friends and doing favors for each other (like giving rides). Hell, seventeen years later, my husband and I still have dinner with Justin and his wife (along with our children). To my recollection, just like Hae and

Adnan, I spearheaded the breakup with Justin. Soon after I, too, obtained a new boyfriend; however, Justin and I remained really good friends. I guess that's why it's not weird to me that people have said that Adnan was a little boastful about having new "chicks" in his life and I've never deemed it strange that he was also simultaneously allowing himself to "be there" for Hae. Teenage relationships are so fickle. I don't believe that we knew back then just how trivial and immature our relationships were. I certainly did not think any of us were willing to kill over them. I didn't realize how inconsistent our relationship ideals were until I came across entries from my own journal from back then. In no particular order, some of them read:

"It's weird being in a relationship and all. Sometimes I love Justin to death, like the air I breathe. Then other times it's like I can't shake him..."

"He's [Justin] independent, yet loyal, loving and sensitive too. Excitable yet self-controlled and sweeter than the sweetest honey...He doesn't bitch when I don't call. We don't argue and he doesn't worry about sex, but instead love. He's real, just like me. I think I'm falling in 'real' love."

"Justin and I are very close, but who knows where we'll be in the future."

"I'm not married to Justin so why do I feel the obligation to be monogamous?"

"By the way, as of 3 weeks ago, me and Justin have been

having an open relationship. I'm thinking of going back to him after the prom."

"As for Justin we ended up drifting apart...maybe I just mistook what ended up being friendship for love."

There is no denying that after reading those entries, I can certainly see how Hae and Adnan's relationship could have been littered with the same type of inconsistencies. After all, when they were dating they did have a sexual relationship and a history of being an "on again, off again couple." I know for a fact that whenever possible, guys like to try and keep that "sex" door propped open. Just in the event that they can "hit it" again in the future. I have seen grown-ass men do the same thing at the end of a relationship. Adnan's attempt doesn't strike me as odd, at all. When Adnan said, "I'm doing my thing," I knew what he meant and I remember hearing that Justin had made the same kind of comments in reference to our breakup. Consequently, I also knew that if I ever needed help from Justin that he, too, was always there for me. So in that regard I took Adnan's comment as a brush-off. When you think about it, all that comment says is, "Whatever, I'm not bothered, I'm getting with other girls anyway," which is pretty typical of a teenage boy who got dumped and is trying to save face. It's also pretty typical and smart of him to tell a cute girl in the library (me) that he just wanted Hae to be happy. That kind of "sweet statement" gets around the teenage girl community quite fast and makes him look good.

Think about it. They say Adnan had already been hooking up with multiple girls by then. Maybe the reason Derrick thought Adnan was trying to holla at me was because he *was?* Maybe I just didn't catch on. I like to think Adnan respected Justin enough to not try to "get with me," but that doesn't mean that he didn't find me attractive and wasn't flirting a little. I think in the podcast Rabia and a close friend of his even said that Adnan was a flirt after his breakup with Hae. In any case, does that sort of talk and behavior seem consistent with someone who cares enough to kill his ex-girlfriend due to jealousy? No, not in my opinion. I suppose anything is possible though.

It was at that moment that I saw Derrick and Jerrod walk in the library behind where Adnan was seated. Adnan turned his head to see who I was looking at and it was at that time that I said, "My ride's here," and got up from the table. I walked over to Derrick and that's when Derrick said, "Who's that?" He instantly puffed out his chest and glared at Adnan as if to silently say, "She's mine." Little did I know that Derrick was cheating on me at the time. I was still so blindly in love and in the dark (but that's another crazy prom story, for another time) that his jealousy made absolutely no sense. I said something like "Nobody" and we left.

It wasn't until we got in the car that Derrick asked me something to the effect of, "Who was that? Was he trying to holla at you?" I chuckled and said, "No! Don't worry about who that was! Nigga, you late as hell!" He then gave me some "side eye" and I just remember Jerrod giggling like a school girl and the fact that I wanted to slap them both. I remember feeling like it was probably Jerrod's fault that Derrick had gotten sidetracked and was late. I remember being pissed that I had waited all that time to now be arguing in the car with Derrick. Not to mention being highly irritated that Jerrod was in the passenger seat of the car and I was seated in the back. Jerrod had refused to give up the passenger seat and Derrick didn't say a word. In any event, I'm not one to hold a grudge so the fight didn't last long. I went to Derrick's house and we continued with our plans.

So that's why I was even at the library to begin with. An inconsiderate high school boyfriend! To this day, I still jokingly give Derrick crap (yes, we're still friends too) about being late. I joke and tell him that my involvement in this case is all his fault. Whenever I think about that encounter, I can't help but wonder how I would have gotten home that day if Derrick hadn't showed. What if Adnan had offered me a ride? Would Hae still be alive? Did Adnan really kill her? Could the same thing have happened to me? What if there was another killer prowling our campus? Could I have been in danger that day? What if Derrick had been on time? Where would Adnan be then? I have been told that I shouldn't ponder such questions because they are depressing and pointless, but I often can't help myself.

So far the most unusual question that has been asked

concerning January 13th is among the ones that haunts me the most. It came across in an online chat that I was in with one of my best friends. We were discussing different aspects of the case and different impressions of Adnan that my friend had from high school. I was giving him my insight into that day in the library. My friend asked about Adnan's demeanor and body language and he asked about conversation details. Just when I thought we had discussed everything that I could remember, my friend asked, "So, do you remember what Adnan was wearing that day? Did he have on a coat or red gloves?" Now, try and try as I may, I can't for the life of me remember what Adnan was wearing. It's like I remember him walking in, seeing his face, catching eye contact and signaling him over to sit down and yet when I try to recall his clothing all I get is a blur. It's like one of those Instagram filters that blurs out the outside edges of your photo. Ever since I experienced that sensation I can't help but feel uneasy about it. It's a very powerless feeling to only be able to see part of a memory in your mind's eye. What's even more unsettling to me is wondering if his attire could provide some insight into his activities that day. What if Adnan was wearing the infamous red leather gloves that he allegedly wore while strangling Hae? What if he was carrying his track bag because he was soon to arrive at track practice? What if Adnan was carrying his cell phone? In any case, my friend thought it was interesting that I couldn't recall that aspect of my memory, and so did I. We eventually abandoned the entire thought as I joked, "Hell, who can even remember what they themselves wore sixteen days ago, let alone what somebody else had on sixteen years ago?" Nevertheless, the absence of that knowledge still does bother me, quite considerably.

One of the more comical speculations that some online commenters have had about me is that I might have harbored a love interest (AKA crush) toward Adnan, and that this crush may have influenced me to lie about being his alibi. At first I just laughed and laughed at the idea—as if I'm some weird Charles Manson-type girlfriend pining for Adnan over the course of sixteen plus years. As if I'm only married with children to pass the time until I can be with Adnan again. I initially thought the idea was a joke, but then I began to realize that some of these people on the Internet were actually serious. Given the seriousness of these accusations, I'd like to take this opportunity to say that I never had a crush on Adnan. When my library conversation took place I was smack in the middle of a three-year relationship with the—then—love of my life. At that point, I had no knowledge of Derrick's infidelity nor did other guys stack up in comparison to Derrick.

After my relationship with Derrick ended, I went on a date with a former classmate who told me that he originally thought I was gay because I had really short hair in high school. My date also said that he thought that because from what he could recall, he could not remember ever seeing me be affectionate with a guy outside of prom night (with Derrick). I had to inform him that the reason for that was that my high school ex-boyfriend was a student of our rival (Milford Mill). I explained that I had been a loyal girlfriend and that's why he never saw me "hugged up" with anyone at our school. Needless to say, I never went out on a date with that guy again! When I see Adnan in my "mind's eye," I don't see him as someone that I've been ever attracted to in the slightest. Not to be mean about it, but let's face facts, from one "schnoz" to another, I have never made a habit of dating my own kind. By that I mean I'm talking about guys with large noses.

In addition, Adnan was pretty sleek back in high school—to what degree I couldn't tell you because I never really scoped him out like that. I do however know that he was far from "beefcake" material. Now Derrick on the other hand. Wow… I'm a happily married woman with children and I can still appreciate some of the memories that I have about Derrick's physique. Do you remember D'Angelo's music video for "Untitled: How Does It Feel?" Well, let's just say that D'Angelo and Derrick shared similar body types back then. To put things into perspective, Derrick and I are both former lifeguards and both of us were both very physically fit in high school. Derrick in particular spent a lot of time swinging from Tarzan ropes at Milford Mill Swim Club quarry and as a result he had a tremendous amount of upper body strength and muscles. I'd even go so far as to describe him as a "hunk" back then. So in comparison, to me Adnan was scrawny and ultimately not my cup of tea. I did have minor attractions to other guys outside of Derrick during my senior year, but I never acted on any of them because I considered myself to be a loyal girlfriend. Adnan, however, was absolutely not one of the guys that I even bothered to look at. On January 13th, I was nice to Adnan because he was nice to me. Plain and simple. I think the reason people have floated the idea of me having a crush on Adnan is because I, along with other people, have often commented about his stellar demeanor, kindness and friendliness. Throughout this whole story that is one of the few consistencies. As Adnan stated himself in the SERIAL podcast, his initial saving grace in terms of public opinion is his personality. By this I mean in the sense that his personality doesn't allude to him being off or some sort of psychopathic murderer. Having had a conversation with Adnan, I can say, if he killed Hae, he would have to be a true psychopath with some real split personality issues. From what I've learned most psychopaths have problems socializing and empathizing with others, to a degree in which it's often quite noticeable. Don't get me wrong, there is still a possibility that Adnan is deeply disturbed. However, over and over again I have encountered many people who knew Adnan and they have all unequivocally said the same thing: "I just don't see him doing something like that."

CHAPTER TWO

'99 TO '00

It's ironic that schoolteachers and parents today focus so much on teaching youth about Internet privacy and how easily videos, pictures and words can go viral. I say this because back then, there wasn't widespread Internet activity and connectivity like today, and yet my little old high school "jail letters" have definitely been made a thing of viral Internet proportions. If only I had known that millions of people would be reading those letters and combing them for evidence of my intentions and character; I probably would have never written them to begin with. Hindsight is indeed twenty-twenty! Such is life, I suppose. You live and you learn. It wasn't until the adults got involved and began meddling with people's words and actions that things got overly complicated. I guess that's the nature of our criminal justice system. Sad thing is, things got so twisted around and neglected that I don't know if we will ever completely know what happened to Hae.

A lot of people have been perplexed by my letters to Adnan back in 1999. When did I write them and why do I mention certain things in the letters? In my defense, I was a teenager and I thought the letters were a lot better than they actually were (and read now). Many people have called into question why I didn't state a specific time in my letters. Why was I so friendly in my letters if I didn't know Adnan? Did I have a crush on Adnan and was I offering to lie for him? Before I address these questions, let me just say this...

I was seventeen, people, geez! None of us were as cunning as you make us out to be. I think many people really have lost sight of the fact that back in 1999 we were all kids. We were all a lot dumber than we realized. Many of the things that I did and wrote were idiotic and many of the things that my schoolmates and I did and said are just plain stupid and nonsensical. None of us knew anything about the real world, let alone what to do when faced with such a heavy situation. Many people online have come down on us all so hard, and I think that's not only extremely harsh but also very hypocritical. Let me ask you something. What were you and your friends doing at seventeen? Did you ever do anything that you weren't supposed to be doing? I venture to say, yes, you did. Now imagine that everyone in the world was to find out about your intimate thoughts and conversations back then. Imagine your daily activities and your very words combed over and analyzed time and time again. Those who live in glass houses shouldn't throw stones, my friend. Ya dig? The thing that I find funniest and most ironic was how complex everyone made us out to be. Jay has become this ultimate criminal mastermind; Adnan led this split personality double life. I've heard everything from Hae being an undercover drug dealer with Jay to me inserting myself into this case for affection from Adnan. At the end of the day, I don't believe anything that we did, said or wrote was that complex and I feel sorry for any adult who thinks that it is. Our teenage life was not a real life reproduction of *Jawbreaker* or *Cruel Intentions*. In relation to my own involvement in this story, everything that I did and wrote was pretty simple when viewed through the lens of a naïve and short-sighted seventeen-year-old girl.

Here's the funny thing about being young: you think you know things that your mind just can't even fully comprehend yet. You have involvement in scenarios with potential consequences that aren't even on your radar yet. That's pretty much how I sum up my "jail letters" to Adnan. At the time, I thought I had a pretty strong grasp on the conveyed intent within my letters. At the time, I thought they conveyed a sense of helpfulness associated with the cautiousness of a potential witness. I gambled that kindness would get me further in relation to getting real case details and maybe, just maybe, if I came off a little friendly that

I'd be given more information about what was going on behind the scenes. Perhaps I could more quickly come to learn what I was volunteering to get involved in. I assumed that if my claims were found to be helpful, then everything would shake out appropriately. I didn't realize that at the time, I was being a young idealistic fool. I didn't know about Cristina Gutierrez's health struggles. Looking back over sixteen years later, I am faced with the evidence that I didn't know shit, that in fact that some people now see my letters as suspiciously vague instead of hesitant. That people now see me as being oddly friendly and overly lighthearted about a really serious situation. In my defense, I have no defense. It is what it was. I was young and not very experienced with death or incarceration correspondence (still am not, thank the Lord). Most of my life I have never had much hesitancy about expressing my thoughts or asking questions. My mother always told me, "You never know unless you ask." So to me, at that moment in time, I didn't understand the futile nature of asking Adnan to dish out case details. Of course I know now that it was an utter and complete waste of time. Especially considering that I was never even questioned by anyone.

Before I describe my letters I must first explain the context in which they were written. I don't remember the specific moment that I realized my library conversation with Adnan was the same day that Hae went missing. I remember hearing that Hae's body had been found in a shallow grave. I recall being disgusted, saddened and shocked along with many of my fellow students. I remember pondering the laziness of her murderer because they couldn't even bother to dig her a proper grave. I remember that for some reason the image of Hae's foot sticking out the ground came to mind—an image that even haunts me today whenever I hear the words "shallow grave" in any context. It wasn't until days after the post-conviction hearing in 2016 that I realized I wasn't alone in having that specific imagery. Many of my Woodlawn magnet friends also share it. It's now my belief that this information must have been one of many rumors swirling around the school at the time Hae's body was discovered.

Upon recently re-listening to the SERIAL podcast (for the second time), I even heard "Mr. S" allude to seeing Hae's foot sticking out of the ground. My best assumption is that this gory detail must have been one of many leaked police sound bites from their student interviews. Either that or someone's over-active imagination just happened to be spot on. When it was discovered that Hae was dead, the entire student body was told to come forward if we had any information that might be helpful. Everyone racked their brains in an effort to recall their last Hae sightings and conversations with her. There wasn't a very high Asian population at Woodlawn, so Hae stood out. Even people who didn't know her were trying to remember seeing her. In this same regard I was no different. However, I could not recall the last time that I had actually seen Hae—only that she had recently been on my mind. After Adnan's arrest, I once again found myself shocked and left wondering about the last time I had seen or spoken to both Hae and Adnan. This was when I remembered having seen and spoken to Adnan on January 13th. Then I recalled that Adnan and I had spoken about Hae that same day. Like Hae's death, the news of Adnan's arrest was all over the high school.

As if the shock of Hae's death wasn't horrible enough, we were faced with the reality that someone that had co-mingled within our company for years was being accused and was possibly responsible for her murder. Naturally there were those who dismissed the possibility, as well as those who thought it was true. Most people that I encountered were either in a state of disbelief or were simply just unsure. I can remember that everyone, students and teachers alike, were pining for more arrest details to come available. This of course only made the rumors swell. By all accounts it was a pretty unproductive few days for everyone. I, too, spent the majority of my school time speculating theories and crowdsourcing opinions and rumors from other students and teachers. After recalling the memory of Adnan in the library, I don't recall if I volunteered that information to anyone at school. Well, not anyone other than Justin Adger and Mr. Parker (my Spanish teacher). I have pictures of the students in Mr. Parker's class and Justin is in them. Perhaps I told both of them at the same time? I don't know for sure. I wasn't the type to interject myself into the high school rumor mill. Especially when it involved something as negative as a murder. I do remember feeling unimportant to the case in the days that followed. The police were already starting to interview students and I was never approached. As you can imagine, this only added to my theory that perhaps the library conversation was of no value. I assumed that between the police interviews, visiting Adnan's family and writing Adnan letters in jail, that my fifteen to twenty minutes spent with Adnan were inconsequential. I wish that I could remember more about those days, but unfortunately my memory has only prevailed so well. I can tell you this much: it was a very disturbing and surreal time for us all.

After Adnan's arrest, I can't say that I was certain that he was capable of murder; however, I assumed that something was going on because he had not been readily released. I wasn't privy to any hard facts, but it was clear the South Asian Muslim and Korean Buddhist communities were pitted against one another from the very start. I soon found myself having a lot of hesitations about speaking up. For one, I didn't know anything about the police's evidence or when they suspected Hae was murdered, so I had no idea if my information would even be relevant. When I think back initially my encounter with Adnan simply seemed creepy more than anything. I remember thinking, "I can't believe I actually talked to Adnan on the same day Hae went missing."

It wasn't until I told this to Justin that it was even highlighted as a possibly important coincidence. Justin recommended that I tell Adnan's family. I initially had my doubts but eventually I agreed that it could be important. Justin had already made plans to visit the Syed family to show support. He asked if I wanted to come with him, so I made plans for him to pick me up and take me to meet Adnan's family. Upon arrival at the Syed home, I was instantly impressed by the sense of community and faith at that house. Everyone was either praying or comforting someone. I was raised Christian, so their strong connection to God in their moment of need was highly impressive. So impressive that I knew I had to speak up and tell the family what I knew. Adnan had just been arrested and emotions were high. As I walked up to the house I remember feeling like one does when approaching a gathering for a funeral wake.

One thing that I will never forget is the level of sorrow in that house. It felt as if someone in their family and/or community had died. I don't know why, but I didn't expect to be so well-welcomed during such an awful time for them, but even prior to my admission, my presence was highly appreciated. They offered me refreshments (soda and cake) and thanked me for what they perceived as a visit to show my support for Adnan. Imagine my state of mind, knowing what I was there to tell them and not knowing if it was even helpful. I remember that they were very grateful for the information because as they had put it, Adnan was having trouble recalling all his actions on January 13th, specifically his activities between school letting out at 2:15 PM and attending his mosque around 8 PM. At the time, I don't think anyone thought that my statement was describing a "murder alibi" for Adnan. I didn't leave feeling like a murder alibi, only that I had helped account or fifteen to twenty minutes of his afternoon. I was just a kid who had given my little part to whittle down that six-hour window. Some people question loyalties, particularly mine, but throughout this whole ordeal, the thought of loyalty to Adnan never even crossed my mind. I never imagined that I would be pegged as part of conspiracy to get Adnan out of jail because I never imagined that what I had to say was even important. After all, until the next day I hadn't encountered anyone who seriously thought that Adnan had committed the murder. I think everyone was still convinced that Adnan's arrest was a mistake and that he would soon be coming home. It was just a matter of closing that remaining window of time, and the police would realize that they had the wrong guy. That's what we all thought at that time.

When I got home later that night, I was filled with such positivity about what I had done. Going to Adnan's house was, again, pretty scary in the sense that I didn't know what to expect. I was relieved that they had been so nice and that the experience was over. I had done my little part and it was presumably done. Everything happened so fast, and my mind had been blown so wide open from the shock of it all. My first thought upon return-ing home that night was to write Adnan a letter to let him know that I had remembered our time together. I didn't know if what I had to say was important, so I didn't know if anyone from the family would tell Adnan. My thought was that if he was having trouble remembering details from his afternoon, then my letter might jog his memory about what he did after I saw him in the library (i.e. if he stayed in the library longer, or ran into another person he knew while there).

I knew Adnan was by all accounts a good kid. At the time, I didn't even know that he was smoking weed in high school. I was also surprised when Adnan tried out for and made the football team (senior year) because I never pegged him as someone that would even have interest in playing football (let alone being good enough to make the team). The thought of him being in jail seemed rough and I knew that I would have been terrified had it been me, so to some degree I wanted to comfort him as well. I was definitely still under the assumption that his arrest was a mistake, but I wasn't 100 percent certain.

As I began to write the letter I realized that I didn't know anything about his arrest. I realized just how unsure I was of Adnan's innocence. All I had was my own wishy-washy suspi-cions and Justin's faith in his friend. In my heart I wanted to think that Adnan was innocent, but in my head I just wasn't sure. Looking back, this was the first time I tried to push the negative possibilities out of my head in order to be neutral in my pursuit of the truth. Some people think my letter language doesn't convey those same sentiments as much as I originally intended, but again, I was only seventeen and not as experienced with writing as I am now. In any case, let's revisit my first letter dated March 1st, 1999, and I will attempt to explain as best I can.

My First Letter: 3/1/1999

it's late

March 1, 1999

I just came from your house an hour ago.

Dear Adnon (I hope I spelled it right). *[I didn't even know how to spell his name correctly!]*

I know that you cant *[have]* visitors *[I was assuming he couldn't have visitors],* so I decided to write you a letter. I'm not sure if you remember talking to me in the library on January 13, but I remember chatting with you. *[attempting to refresh his memory in the event he forgot]* Throughout your actions that day *[how nicely he spoke about Hae]* I have reason to believe in your innocence. *[referring to his candor at the library when discussing the breakup and because Justin vouched for his character]* I went to your family's house and discussed your "calm" manner towards them. *[His family was shocked by the arrest; I told them about my conversation with Adnan and that he seemed calm on January 13th]* also called the Woodlawn Public Library and found out that they have a surveillance system inside the building. *[Called the library, the person answering the phone confirmed the presence of security cameras]* Depending on the amount of time you spend in the library that afternoon, it might help your defense. *[Perhaps he stayed at the library longer; maybe he spoke to someone else that could account for more time]* I really would appreciate it if you contact me between 1:00pm - 4pm or 8:45pm -->until... My number is XXX-XXX-XXXX. *[best time to reach me, most days]*

More importantly I'm trying to reach your lawyer, to schedule a possible meeting with the three of us. *[It was Sunday, so not possible—good intentions or short attention span at most; never happened]* We aren't really close friends, but I want you to look me into my eyes and tell me of your innocence. *[I was having trouble reconciling our library conversation with the thought of Adnan being a murderer. I was dumb enough to think that perhaps if he told me he was innocent to my face, I could read him for guilt or innocence.]* If I ever find out otherwise, I will hunt you down and whip your ass, okay friend *[trying to lighten the fact that I just threatened to potentially whip his ass]* I hope you're not guilty and I hope to God that you have nothing to do with it *[being unsure]*. If so I will try my best to help you account for some *[Some, not all! Only 15-20 minutes!]* of your own unwitnessed unaccountable time (2:15-8pm Jan 13th). *[Being overly descriptive. I was not trying to be vague about the amount of time I was willing to vouch for]* The police have not been notified yet to my knowledge. *[Hadn't spoken to the police as of that night, but I was considering it. I eventually attempted to call them but chickened out after dialing the phone number. As a teenager, the general consensus was that Baltimore copes were not to be trusted so I didn't know if going to them first was the best thing to do.]* Maybe it will give your side of the story a particular head start *[Alluding to his possible innocence and hoping this information leads to other helpful memories/information]* I hope that you appreciate this, seeing as though I would like to stay out of this whole thing *[being honest]*. Thank Justin, he gave me a little bit more faith in you. Through his friendship and faith. I'll pray for you and that the "real truth" *[perhaps his arrest is all just a horrible mistake]* comes out in the end. I hope it will set you free *[physically if innocent, mentally if guilty and he confesses]*. Only trying to help,

Asia McClain

Ps: If necessary my grandparents number is DO NOT call that line after 11:00 OK

Like I told Justin, if you're innocent I will do my best to help you. But if you're not only God can help you.

If you weren't *[were, not weren't]* in the library for a while, tell the police and I'll continue to tell what I know even louder than I am. *[Asking if he stayed in the library for some time after I left, to notify police and I will tell the truth about seeing him during the 15-20 minutes that I did].*

My boyfriend and his best friend remember seeing you there too. *[Before writing the letter I confirmed with Derrick and Jerrod if they remembered seeing Adnan in the library and at the time they did, so I wanted Adnan to know that it wasn't just me who knew that he was there during that 15-20 minutes]*

Your Amiga *[being nice]*

Asia McClain

"Look into my eyes and tell me of your innocence" sound pretty lame and cheesy right? I agree; that was my seventeen-year-old attempt to be dramatic. Part of me still feels like that is something that I really still need Adnan to do. I even alluded to that sentiment in my *Good Morning America* interview, after Adnan's post-conviction hearing in early 2016 (I don't think they aired that part). Sitting here today, I can still say that I strongly feel like that is something he should do. Being involved in this case has always been uncomfortable to me. Adding all the publicity from the SERIAL podcast and the post-conviction hearing certainly made it much more stressful. The feeling of assisting someone who may very well be a murderer is an unsettling realization that I have come to accept.

The thing that I can't ever accept is the sorrow associated with being wedged between two families—both seeking justice for their lost children, both hurting and both looking to me to do the right thing. At best, I try to tell myself not to focus on Adnan's guilt or innocence, rather instead just to do my job as a witness and tell the truth. Regardless of that simplistic approach, it's often very hard to stay focused and during those times the weight of the situation gets to me (and I break down and cry). Just to be clear, I haven't seen Adnan (outside of the post-conviction hearing in 2016) since that fortuitous day in the library. Other than maybe speaking with him very briefly when this is all over, I have no desire to ever speak with him again. I have no desire to be his friend and I don't want to keep in touch. When I recall our library conversation, the memory still haunts me to this day. While in the moment, I truly believed that he was a sweet guy. As I said before, Justin and I parted on similar terms, so perhaps in my heart I wanted to believe that Adnan and Justin shared a similar sense of maturity and kindness. At the time I believed that Adnan cared about Hae and that he simply wanted her to be happy with whomever she chose to be in a relationship with. If Adnan was under emotional duress to the point of being homicidal, I feel like I should have seen it. I know that's a silly thing to say, but I have a very hard time accepting that he was homicidal during or shortly after we spoke. Clearly I didn't see anything wrong with him, otherwise I definitely would have told someone. The idea that he was or became homicidal as a result of our conversation scares the crap out of me because it makes me wonder if I am somehow responsible for Hae's death.

I often wonder if I didn't see evil in him because it wasn't there or if it was because I was a dumb kid. Perhaps the reason that I didn't realize something was going on under the surface was because I was too young and naïve. At seventeen, I wasn't experienced enough with evil people at that point in my life. I've always thought I was able to read people, but perhaps not.

Since high school I have had the pleasure of knowing some pretty dysfunctional people. My mom says that I'm a "nut magnet." She says that I have a beautiful light inside of me that shines and unfortunately like a moth to flame it attracts those living in the darkness. After looking back on my twenties I'd have to say that I agree with my mother. Sometimes I'm amazed that I have managed to come through certain situations so unscathed. I know that I am blessed and that I can only attribute that to my mother's many prayers and the presence of the Holy Spirit in my life. I've seen people abuse themselves and abuse others, and yet I have managed to stay clear of many awful situations.

During the times when I have fallen prey to negative situations, it is my belief that God was there to pull me out. It's also during those times that God showed me "the writing on the wall"; I paid attention to the words and actions around me and I was often alerted to trouble before things got too damaging to recover from. Long story short: I wasn't as wise as I am now in any regard. Real life murder wasn't even something that truly existed in my reality at the age of seventeen. Consequently, I do feel like Adnan owes me. He doesn't owe me money or gratitude; he owes me the truth and I hope one day whether here or in Heaven, I get it.

If you haven't caught on by now, I have a very active imagination. Over the years I have imagined having this final conversation with Adnan many times, in a variety of ways. In one scenario Adnan gets acquitted and agrees to meet me. We meet at a public park bench and he thanks me for ultimately coming forward and being the person who saved him from a life in prison. He tells me everything that's happened since his arrest and I am silent in amazement regarding everything that he has endured. Then we both shed tears over Hae's untimely passing, share a few sentiments and he assures me that he never had anything to do with Hae's disappearance or her murder. I cry knowing that I have done an awesome thing and for a deserving person. I heave a deep sigh of relief in knowing that an innocent man has been set free in part by me choosing to do the right thing. As we part ways he asks to hug me, and I oblige. Then I see him walk off into the distance arm in arm with members of his family. Now, I know that seems corny and lame to most people, but I would totally cry if I saw that in a movie!

The other scenarios are much darker. These scenarios are reserved solely for my nightmares. In them, sometimes Adnan is acquitted and shows up on my doorstep to seemingly innocently thank me for my help. I'm home alone and he pushes his way inside my home. I run for my weapon of choice, but he's too fast. A struggle ensues during which not only does he confess to Hae's murder but casually mentions that I'm next. He climbs on top of my body in an attempt to hold me down. He bangs the back of my head on the floor and as I lay there struggling for my life, he tells me about every horrible detail of Hae's murder. He wraps his hands around my throat and begins to squeeze. I struggle to fight for my life as I feel myself tiring. It's at these moments in the nightmare that I usually wake up in a cold sweat. Dreams like these are my primary motivation for self-defense and target practicing. Other dreams and scenarios that I have imagined combine Adnan's innocence or guilt with him getting out of or staying in jail. Sometimes, I have similar dreams about Jay Wilds.

In one dream, Adnan isn't acquitted and after many years in prison I receive a call from Justin Brown (his lawyer) saying that Adnan wants to see me. Like that of any other typical jailhouse visitation scene we both sit down at a metal table and chair to talk. He tells me that he asked me here to address something in one of my letters. It's then that Adnan confesses his guilt to me and thanks me for my participation in his release efforts. Disgusted by what I have just heard, I abruptly stand up and proceed to leave the facility both sickened and ashamed. As I run out, tears running down my face, I grasp my open mouth in complete horror, and Adnan laughs hysterically in a fit of insanity in the background. Now I know these thoughts and nightmares may or may not seem strange for someone in my legal position, however you have to realize that I have had way too much time to stress about this situation. Sixteen plus years is a long time to waver and weigh in on another person's guilt or innocence. I have over sixteen years of stress, over sixteen years of preponderance and over sixteen years of thoughts built up in my subconscious mind. I don't know if I will ever actually speak to Adnan again and part of me is fine with that because I'm a little scared to. In January 2015 I did ask my lawyer (Gary Proctor) to ask Justin Brown about the possibility of speaking to Adnan when this was all over. I don't know if Gary ever relayed my question. Even though I did ask, I'm not even entirely sure that I wouldn't be too scared and chicken out. One part of me feels like I need that type of closure and part of me feels like I never will, regardless of what Adnan has to say. I don't think there will ever come a day when I can go to bed at night not wondering if I've helped a murderer.

Back in 1999 my family was one of few in our neighborhood to have a home PC. That was back in the days of AOL (dial-up Internet) and I had to share my upstairs phone line with a PC located in the basement. On many occasions I would use that computer to type school assignments among other things. My best guess is that because I wrote my first letter to Adnan so late that night that it was probably too late to gain access to my grandparents' PC in the basement. In my grandparents' home, the basement was (and always will be) my grandfather's man cave. As such, access to it by teenagers was undesirable after a certain time at night because my grandfather would (and still does) fall asleep in his armchair. It only makes sense to me that I would have written the letter by hand in my bedroom if it were indeed very late at night. This also explains why letter number two was typed. As I stated at the post-conviction hearing in 2016, I wrote the rough draft of letter number two over the course of that next school day. Since I neglected to ask a lot of questions in my first letter, I made it a point to ask a lot more when I typed up my second letter. I took great care to formally address the letter as taught to me in school and made sure to include lots (too much) of quirky clipart. At no point was letter number two backdated and at no point did Adnan ever contact me and encourage me to write him anything. As an attempt to debunk this conspiracy theory I tried to get my grandparents' old PC to see if I could locate the original computer file. Unfortunately for me, after seventeen years not only were my grandparents not even using it as a bookend (in the basement) anymore, they no longer even owned that PC block at all. As a family that still has VCRs and lava lamps in the basement, I was both pretty surprised and pissed that they no longer had it.

Another conspiracy theory that arose about letter number

two came straight from the mouth of Thiru Vignarajah himself, during the post-conviction in 2016. During his cross-examination of my testimony Vignarajah accused me of using terminology in my letter that could be found on Adnan's original search warrant. He insinuated that someone (presumably Adnan) had spoon-fed me the information resulting in the second letter to Adnan. Thiru squawked that Adnan had written me with instructions to type him a letter for his bail review and possibly as an alibi. Thiru tied this accusation to the fact that I knew Adnan's inmate number (probably given to me by the Syed family, a teacher or friend), along with other words within my letters. These accusations caught me completely off guard for a plethora of reasons, the primary reason being that of course they were untrue. I have never received any communication from Adnan since that day in the library. No one has ever given me specific instructions to write him anything. I can't sit here and tell you that Adnan didn't try to write me back. All I can account for is the fact that I have never received any correspondence from Adnan in any fashion.

As I sit here today I still haven't seen the warrant document that Thiru brought up in court. I also could not tell you the details of its contents. The second and more obvious reason that I found his line of questioning to be off-putting was that he was essentially calling me a liar and co-conspirator to my face. Even after the post-conviction hearing he continued to call me a liar on the news. I found that to be very insulting, spirit-crushing and enraging all at the same time.

What a horrible precedent this case has set in terms of encouraging witnesses to come forward with helpful information. A person such as myself, with no criminal record and no motive to lie, comes forward to tell the truth and the prosecution pounces on her. The state calls her a liar and attempts to ruin her good name both in court and in the press. I can understand a prosecutor wanting to win his case, but at what cost? I still think a lot of Thiru's actions inside and outside of the courtroom are downright crude and sleazy to say the least. I can openly admit that I have been scarred by my participation in this case. For the time being, I no longer see the state as a faction of the court that cares about the truth. To me, it feels like they only care about winning. Thanks to Urick and Vignarajah, I can wholeheartedly say that it will be a long time before I ever trust a state prosecutor (aka "The Good Guys") again and that's just really sad.

My Second Letter: 3/2/1999

Adnon Syed *[name spelled wrong again]* #992005477 *[no clue how I got his inmate number—family? Friends?]*

301 East Eager Street

Baltimore, MD. 21202

Dear Adnon, *[still spelled his name wrong]*

How is everything? I know that we haven't been best friends in the past, however I believe in your innocence. *[after more contemplation and general public consensus]* I know that central booking *[no idea where this verbiage came from—possibly school gossip]* is probably not the best place to make friends, so I'll attempt to be the best friend possible. I hope that nobody has attempted to harm you *[beat him up in jail]* (not that they will). Just remember that if someone says something to you, that their just f**ing with your emotions. I know that my first letter was probably a little harsh, but I just wanted you to know where I stode *[stood]* in this entire issue (on the centerline) *[not necessarily on his side]*. I don't know you very well, however I didn't know Hae very well. The information that I know about you being in the library could helpful, unimportant or unhelpful to your case *[still not aware of the state's argument or that my information is important in terms of being an alibi]*. I've been think a few things lately, that I wanted to ask you: *[Primary reason for writing a second letter the very next day—could not reconcile Adnan's demeanor with the thought of him being a murderer and had more questions as a result.]*

1. Why haven't you told anyone about talking to me in the library? Did you think it was unimportant, you didn't think that I would remember? Or did you just totally forget yourself? *[Wanted to know if he had forgotten about the encounter or whether the encounter itself was insignificant. Many students were being interviewed by the police and I had not been chosen to*

be interviewed yet.]

2. How long did you stay in the library that day? Your family will probably try to obtain the library's surveillance tape. *[Wondering how long after our conversation he stayed at the library. I think I mentioned to the family that there might be cameras and that they should see if Adnan stayed at the library after I left—could be why their private investigator went to the library but did not call me. Remember, no one knew I was the alibi at that point. I was assuming that someone would grab the videotape to check.]*

3. Where exactly did you do and go that day? What is the so-called evidence that my statement is up against? And who are these WITNESSES? *[I heard that there were witnesses in conjunction to his arrest—no idea how many because I was going off of rumor. Here, I'm trying to anticipate whether my information would be well received by the police or if they would be hostile towards me because I might be making their case harder to prove. Back then, I had an irrational fear of the police because of stories from friends.]*

Anyway, everything in school is somewhat the same. The ignorant (and some underclassmen) think that you're guilty, while others (mostly those that know you) think you're innocent. I talked to Emron *[was actually spelled "Imran" or "Imraan," not sure (now) which person I was referencing here because there were two guys]* today, he looked like crap. He's upset, most of your "CRUCHES are." *[people who defended Adnan and were supportive and uplifting]* We love you, *[being nice]* I guess that inside I know that you're innocent too. *[wanting to believe in his innocence]* It's just that the so-called evidence looks very negative. *[no idea about actual evidence, just what was rumored]* However I'm positive that everything will work out in favor of the truth. *[not his innocence but the truth—still not sure if he is guilty or not]* The main thing that I'm worried about is that the real killers *[whoever, if it's not Adnan—could be one or more]* are probably somewhere laughing at the police and the news, that makes me sick!! I hope this letter and the ones that follow *[never wrote again because I assumed I was of no use and so I went on with my life]* ease you days a little. I guess if I didn't believe in your innocence, that I wouldn't write to you .

The other day (Monday) *[being specific, I put Monday in parentheses because I was assuming he wouldn't get the letter for a few days and I wanted him to know what day was "the other day." I have no idea why I didn't just structure the sentence differently.]* We (some of Mr. Parker's class) were talking about it and Mrs. Shab over-heard us; she said, "Don't you think the police have considered everything, they wouldn't just lock him up unless they had "REAL" evidence." We just looked at her, then continued our conversations. Mr. Parker seems un-opinionated, yet he seemed happy when I told him *[on Tuesday]* that I spoke to you family about the matter (I told him) *[I told Mr. Parker about seeing Adnan in the library and about talking to Adnan's family, but on two separate days. The wording here is horrible*

*because it reads as if these two conversations happened the same
day but they did not. One conversation happened in class on
Monday, the other in the hallway on Tuesday. When I saw Mr.
Parker in the hallway on Tuesday and told him that I had actually gone to see Adnan's family, he was proud of me for speaking
up.]* Your brothers are nice, I don't think I met your mother
[not sure if I met her or not], I think I met you dad; does he have
a big gray beard *[not sure who all I met because there were a lot
of people there]*. They gave me and Justin soda and cake. There
was a whole bunch of people at you house, I didn't know they
were. I also didn't know that Muslins take their shoes off in
the house...thank God they didn't make me take mine off, my
stinky feet probably would have knocked everyone out cold.
[all this refers to the night before at the family's house]

I over-heard Will and Anthony *[fellow football players]* talking
about you, they don't think you did "IT" either. I guess most
people don't. Justin's mom is worried about you too. She gave
me your home number, when Justin was in school. *[I don't
remember that]* Classes are boring, that's one benefit to being
"there" *[in jail]*, no school!!

They issued a school newsletter *[I think it was actually just a
flyer statement.]* on the issue, so everyone is probably aware. It
didn't say your name, but between that, gossip and the news,
your name is known. I'm sorry this had to happen to you.
Look at the bright side when you come back *[to school]*, won't
nobody f**k with you *[because he had been in jail]* and at least

you'll know who your real friends and new friends should be. *[those being supportive]* Also, you're the most popular guy in school. Shoot...you might get prom king. *[assuming he would be released soon and everyone would know who he is because of all the gossip—it's a joke]*

You'll be happy to know that the gossip is dead for your associates, *[people who don't know Adnan well]* starting to get old. *[my opinion of the repetitive nature of high school gossip and how quickly the talk gets old when there is no new information]* Your real friends are concentrated on you and your defense. *[not referring to myself, rather his crutches]* I want you to know that I'm missing the instructions of Mrs. Ogle's CIP class, writing this letter. *[Wrote it during class and made a decision to keep it in the final draft because I thought it sounded cool for some weird reason. Dumb, I know.]*

It's weird, since I realized that I saw you in the public library that day, you've been on my mind. The conversation that we had, has been on my mind. Everything was cool that day, maybe if I would have stayed with you or something this entire situation could have been avoided. *[wondering if I had stayed at the library longer I could have served as a potential alibi, not realizing that I was his alibi]* Did you cut school that day? Someone told me that you cut school to play video games at someone's house. *[rumor]* Is that what you told the police? This entire case puzzles me, you see I have an analytical mind. I want to be a criminal psychologist for the FBI one day. I don't understand how it took the police three weeks to find Hae's car, if it was found in the same park. *[rumored]* I don't understand how you would even know about Leakin Park *[I didn't even know where Leakin Park was until 2016]* or how the police expect you to follow Hae in your car, kill her and take her car to Leakin Park, dig a grave and find you way back home. *[speculation based on rumors]* As well how come you don't have any markings on your body from Hae's struggle. *[My classmates and I discussed this and then asked one another if we remembered Adnan having any abnormal markings in the last few weeks. No one did.]* I know that if I was her, I would have struggled. *[Adnan would have been hurt if I was the victim. I would have fought back. I think Hae would have, too.]* I guess that's where the SO-CALLED witnesses *[not sure if there were really witnesses or if that was just a rumor]*. White girl Stacie *[not a friend of mine]* just mentioned that she thinks you did it. Something about your fibers on Hae's body... something like that (evidence) *[one of the many rumors floating around school]*. I don't mean to make you upset talking about it...if I am. *[telling him that he is a topic of gossip]* I just thought that maybe you should know. *[so that he would be prepared for all the rumors when he came back]* Anyway I have to go to third period *[the bell had rung and I needed to report to co-op before leaving school for the day]*. I'll write you again. Maybe tomorrow. *[never did write again]*

Hope this letter brightens your day... Your Friend,

Asia R. McClain

P.S: Your brother said that he going to tell you to maybe call me, it's not necessary, save the phone call for your family. *[I still wanted Adnan to contact me but I was attempting to be considerate of the fact that his phone calls may have been limited in prison]* You could attempt to write back though. So I can tell everyone how you're doing (and so I'll know too).

Asia R. McClain (address)

Apparently a whole bunch of girl were crying for you at the jail. *[It was rumored that a bunch of girls were so upset that they actually tried to visit him in jail but were denied visitation]* Big Playa Playa (ha ha ha he he he). *[just trying to be funny]*

My Original Affidavit

As much as it shames me to admit this, in the months after Adnan's arrest, our student life simply went on. Adnan was arrested on the last day of February in 1999. In the months that followed my classmates and I became obsessed with fun senior traditions, prom, graduation and getting settled into college life. We all cared for Hae and wondered about Adnan from time to time, but it was a sore subject that we all tended to steer clear of discussing. In all honesty, it often still feels like the elephant in the room whenever the case is in the news again (all these years later). I do remember feeling a little insulted that Adnan never wrote me back from jail because I had heard rumors that other people had received letters. Eventually I just told myself, "So what? It's not like we were really friends anyway."

As more time went on I assured myself that he was probably focused on more important people and things. I also figured there must have been a reason for the lack of contact. I began to assume that perhaps my time with him on January 13th was not important. It's even possible that I assumed that perhaps I had mailed the letters to the wrong address. Then I began to assume that Adnan *was* Hae's killer and that perhaps the murder took place later on January 13th or a different day all together. Considering that I didn't follow the case and it wasn't something that my friends and I discussed, my assumptions became my truth.

Ever since my letters and affidavits have been made available on the Internet, many people have had their own speculations and questions about my wording choices. My 2000 handwritten affidavit is no exception. Why is the handwriting so different? Why was one document handwritten, while another was typed and so on? All I can say is that they are what they are. I will attempt to explain as best as I can but ultimately it's all just a fascinating coincidence. As with many people my handwriting changes depending on my writing circumstances. What I'm writing, where I'm writing and with what sort of writing instrument I am using plays a major part in how my handwriting looks. I myself have four different signatures that I use depending on the magnitude of my laziness in any particular moment. As many moms can relate, you put me in a retail store with my two toddlers and you're lucky if you can get my initials legibly.

In terms of my original affidavit the majority of the negative speculation surrounds the sentence "We [Adnan and I] talked about his girlfriend [Hae] and he seemed very calm and caring." To many folks it seems rather suspicious that I would include such a sentimental description of my conversation with Adnan. To many it may seems like this wording may have been orchestrated (by Rabia) to make Adnan sound more docile or innocent. To some degree I would have to agree with you; however, Rabia had nothing to do with it. When I wrote that description, I intended to describe Adnan as simply what I did, calm and caring. Its original intention was to convey a greater sense of acceptance of Adnan's demeanor in reference to the breakup. It also happens to be true that, to me, Adnan seemed very unfazed and compassionate about Hae's love life choices. Rabia didn't need to coach that sentiment out of me. It was already a sentiment that I had taken from my actual conversation with Adnan on January 13th.

During the post-conviction hearing in 2016, prosecutor Thiru Vignarajah stated that Rabia testified that she called me after Syed's conviction in early 2000. He also claimed that the purpose of her call was to schedule a time to ask me questions about January 13th, 1999. As I sat in court that day in 2016, I could not remember that phone conversation ever taking place. I did testify to the feeling of surprise when Rabia arrived at my door. I don't know if perhaps there was another reason for remembering a sense of surprise by her visit. Who knows, this was me in the midst of testifying, attempting to recall a memory from seventeen years prior. Perhaps she was different than I expected. Perhaps she was shorter or prettier than I anticipated. Perhaps she arrived late or early. Perhaps it was because she may not have been alone when she arrived. I can't tell you. What I can say is that in the days after testifying I began to remember glimmers of speaking to Rabia on the phone. It began to feel like a small crack had opened up in the memory vault in my mind. I started to have the feeling that a phone conversation did take place with Rabia and that maybe I was in the kitchen making food when she had called. I'm not sure. The feeling was and still is very eerie to me, because I'm not certain about it and I've never been able to recall anything concrete.

I have racked my brain over and over trying to remember something definitive, however nothing comes to mind. I can only assume that I didn't hold on to that memory because to me the conversation wasn't important. The point of the conversation was for her to schedule a visit and the actual visit is what was important to me and what I remember. It is also being thrown around that Rabia testified at the first post-conviction hearing that she, Saad and I also visited the Woodlawn Public Library in addition to going to see the notary. This could be true; I don't remember. I can only remember going to the notary and I don't remember anyone else being in the car. Again, this is after asking me how many years later?

It was a beautiful, warm spring day when Rabia parked her car outside my grandparents' house. I remember thinking that it was a dirty, unappealing little car, maybe blue (I'm not sure and I can't exactly ask). The outside was dirty and I remember that she had a lot of papers inside of it. Either way I recall not liking her car and feeling kind of suspicious about her legitimacy as an attorney because of it. I also remember talking to her outside on the porch. She was a stranger and I was not about to invite a stranger into my home while alone. Female or not. I had been a "latch and key kid" from a very early age, and "no strangers in the house" was a cardinal rule that I never broke. I remember feeling confused about the purpose of Rabia's visit because I did not follow the Syed trial and my knowledge of all the evidence heard by the jury was non-existent. As such I remember initially feeling quite guarded when Rabia showed up. I do remember that she was very polite and that I was the one who was somewhat a little rude and impatient. I had made plans to go somewhere that day and she was holding me up. I remember contemplating whether or not I should write the affidavit because I wasn't sure to what degree I was volunteering to re-involve myself with the case. At some point I recall essentially saying to myself, "Screw it. What's the worst thing that could happen? He's already in prison." I knew it was the right thing to do, so I went with my gut and agreed to write the affidavit anyway. Rabia grabbed a sheet of paper and wrote the word "Affidavit" at the top. She then handed me that same sheet of paper along with a pen. As I grabbed them from her I said, "Okay, now what?" and she responded by telling me to just repeat what I had just told her verbally in the affidavit. It was at this point I reminded Rabia that I had never written an affidavit before and that I didn't know how to start it. She suggested that I start by stating my name, that I was of sound mind, my age and where I was previously and currently attending school. It made sense to me to do so, for identification and legitimacy purposes, so I obliged.

Many people have speculated that Rabia spoon-fed me important times to relay in my first affidavit but this is simply not true. I don't even recall Rabia telling me when the state had theorized that Adnan had killed Hae. Perhaps that she thought I was already aware. Perhaps she thought I understood the importance of the affidavit that I was writing, (call me naïve or stupid) but at the time I did not. In the affidavit I repeated the story of my chance encounter with Adnan Syed. While writing, I recalled that Woodlawn had already let out for the day at 2:15 PM. I also recalled that all the school buses were about to take the majority of students off the school property, thus why I wrote 2:20 PM in parentheses in the affidavit. I stated the amount of time that Adnan and I spent together and our location, along with a brief description of Adnan's demeanor. Towards the end of writing the affidavit Rabia once again asked if I was sure that no one from Syed's legal team had ever contacted me, to which I replied "yes." This seemed to be of great importance to her (because she had asked me multiple times throughout our conversation) so I made sure to include a statement referring to that fact at the end of my affidavit.

When it came to signing the affidavit, I remember that I did have the fleeting thought of waiting until an adult came home before signing it. I wasn't quite sure when that would be, so instead of waiting (because I had other plans) I made the decision to go ahead and sign the affidavit without waiting. This is when Rabia especially annoyed me. I was ready to end the conversation thinking that my duty was almost complete. Rabia then informed me that my signature needed to be witnessed and signed by a notary. Again, this highly annoyed me because I had somewhere else to be and considered it a huge inconvenience of my time to have to leave with Rabia to get the notarization done. I don't remember exactly where the notary was located; I believe at a check-cashing place at a local shopping center. I have read online that the notary location had been criticized. Why didn't Rabia take me somewhere more official like a bank? Best answer

I can give you is that A) the banks were closed and B) she was trying to get me somewhere close and quick because she could tell that my patience was running low.

So into her little car we went. The fact that I was getting into the car of a stranger did cross my mind, however it was another fleeting thought that I eventually shook off. As I got into her car I remember thinking that I could "hold my own" if she began to drive me anywhere other than where we'd discussed. Funny thing is after she began to drive, I remember checking to see if my passenger door was unlocked (and it was), in the event that I needed to jump out of her moving car. Yeah, I thought I was pretty badass back then. The thought of road rash was something I was willing to take over being kidnapped and possibly murdered any day. Luckily Rabia was cool and we didn't have any issues that required me to activate my "badassdom." You'd think I'd remember more about the notary experience itself but I do not. Probably because I was in a rush to get it over with. It was my first time ever having a document notarized but I don't remember the exact location or the person who notarized it. I do remember that it wasn't too long of a drive from my house and that I was perplexed after Rabia accidentally drove past my house (by about two houses) when she attempted to drop me back off at home. I remember thinking, "Really? Weren't you just here, lady?" and then she, embarrassed, apologized for her error.

The last thing that I recall about the whole situation was that it immediately felt like Rabia was going to hug and kiss me all over my face after the document was "official." I remember her being very happy and thankful, kind of like the type of thankfulness you'd imagine getting when returning a lost child. In any case I remember that her reaction made me feel good inside. As I went to close the door, I stopped and said, "Oh, my boyfriend and his buddy Jerrod remember seeing Adnan that day too. They aren't the type to want to get involved with cops and court stuff, so don't involve them unless you have to. I know they remember because I asked them before I wrote those letters." Rabia agreed and then she left. Looking back, I wish I had never told Rabia to hold off on contacting them. Perhaps she could have gotten them to sign affidavits. Then, them not remembering now would be a nonissue. In any case, it would be many many years before I would come to understand the true gravity of that affidavit, but for the time being I had done something that made her very happy and that made me feel good.

After The Affidavit

As much as I hate to admit it, Rabia's visit was soon forgotten. In all honesty Adnan became the furthest person from my mind. Things between Derrick and I had become excessively strained due to his constant run-ins with the law. After being together for a couple of years, Derrick mysteriously disappeared one day for a few weeks. Like Jerrod and many of Derrick's other friends I was concerned, more so downright distraught, at his sudden disappearance. Unfortunately for me in particular (being his girlfriend) Derrick's mother wasn't giving anybody any answers. Several weeks went by (over a month) only for me to find out that he was being held captive at his grandmother's home on house arrest. I never figured out if it was an official or family-induced house arrest but either way he wasn't allowed to leave her home. In any case, I wasn't supposed to know where he was, therefore I definitely wasn't allowed to visit him or speak to him on the phone.

In addition to this relationship drama, I was a new student at Catonsville Community College. Back then, I was completely unsure of what I wanted to do with my life. Like most young adults that age, I was very indecisive about all the educational and career paths that lay before me. All my friends (the magnet kids) were attending state colleges like UMBC and had their academic majors outlined and figured out. For the first time I felt completely and utterly alone, which only added to my hatred of my college experience. As a consequence, I had cultivated a handful of new friends, none of whom were really doing anything with their lives and I just felt as if I was going down a bad path. I worked part-time as a sales assistant at the Clinique Cosmetics counter at the Security Square Hecht's Department Store. I was very unhappy with the way things were going.

Community college was not a good place for me. I think like my magnet friends I needed the "full college experience" and the lack of that experience was causing me to rapidly lose interest in school all together. Community college felt like it was full of strangers, I felt alone and like I did not fit in anywhere. I can remember walking around campus with my earphones on, now equating that experience to that of Star-Lord, on an alien planet. For the first time I felt like a loner.

It wasn't until December 1999 when one of my best friends, Stacie Allen, came home for her winter break. She was attending an out of state college that she loved but was having some issues with on-campus housing. As a result, she wanted to get an off-campus apartment. She didn't have any volunteers for roommates and her father was not comfortable with the idea of her staying alone off-campus and out of state. Once I told her how things were going for me, she invited me to come live off-campus with her in an apartment. I thought about the offer and considering I could attend community college anywhere I decided to go out of state with her. The following spring break, I visited her, made some new friends and soon after we found an apartment. I began to make plans to relocate to my life the following summer. Just a few months before all of this I had signed the first affidavit. I soon forgot all about Adnan, Rabia and the affidavit, as I was dealing with all the challenges that come along with living on my own, out of state for the first time.

Once I moved, nothing went according to plan and I experienced a lot of turmoil, personally and financially—issues that would consume my life and attention for the following six and a half years. I can admit now, much of my stress was self-inflicted, the result of my determination and stubbornness to remain independent of my family.

CHAPTER THREE

2010

During the spring of 2010, a lot was going on in my life. My husband Phillip and I had been recently married and we were adjusting to sharing our lives together. I was adjusting to life as stay-at-home wife and business owner. There were many personal and financial issues at play within our household. At the time we were living in a beautiful 1,600-square foot, three-story townhouse in the Lions Gate community, located in Hillsboro, Oregon. Money was a little tight because of the one-income situation and I had been having some extremely stressful health issues as a result of my battle with Ulcerative Colitis. To make matters worse, my husband and I were in the midst of finding new employers so that we could move over 365 miles to another state, in order to start our family and be closer to my husband's family. Neither of us had close relatives in Oregon so having family nearby was our most viable option for having kids. As I always say, "You got to go where the babysitters are!"

In addition to all of this stress, we were also in the midst of trying to build our own business and planning our (delayed) wedding ceremony in July of that year. All in all, our life together was at a major crossroads and we were going through some major life events, which are all known to measure pretty high on the Holmes and Rahe Stress Scale. I say this not to make excuses for my actions, rather to paint a more accurate view of my life in 2010 so it can be better understood. Nevertheless, things were touchy but overall I considered my life with Phillip to be pretty blessed. I still do. One thing that made the stress all worth it was that I was in love with a man who absolutely adored me (and still does) and we were hand-in-hand embarking on the journey of our lives. Like I said before, I've had my share of negative relationships. For the first time there were no unhealthy friendships in my life nor were there any hints of drama that often accompanies such people. So when the private investigator showed up looking for me, it was an unpleasant reminder of the type of drama that I had worked so hard to eliminate in my life. All in all, it was not a far stretch to say that I was downright rattled by the investigator's presence outside of my home.

It was a normal day by all accounts and my husband was away for a business meeting. I was upstairs on the third floor of the townhome doing laundry. As it has been since explained to me, my husband pulled his blue Honda Accord into the driveway and proceeded to walk up to the house when he was stopped by a female stranger. After introducing herself the investigator explained that she was looking for a young woman by the name of Asia McClain, in reference to a trial from 2000. According to my husband, his hands were overloaded with materials from his car, so he politely asked to be excused for a moment, in order to "put down his belongings." He quickly came inside and by this time I was on the second floor of the townhome in the kitchen. He quickly ran up the stairs to where I was now sitting on the couch. As he gasped for air he said, "Hey babe, there's a private investigator outside asking for you by your maiden name. I think it's about that girl that got murdered when you were in high school." As soon as I heard those words vacate his mouth and saw the perplexing look on his face, I felt a rush of adrenaline shoot through my body. Perhaps it was hearing him say the words "murdered" or "private investigator" but I freaked out. By this point in my life, I'd had my fair share of negative experiences with people "finding me." Some of these included people who often tried to follow me home (years before) in order to steal my sports car and an ex-boyfriend who had trouble letting go. So a strange person showing up at my house rudely (said my husband) and spouting off words like "murder" didn't exactly stimulate immediate reciprocity from me.

"What?!" I said. A flood of thoughts raced through my head.

How did they find where I lived? The Internet was by no means as awesome as it is now. Plus, I was newly married (with a new name) and I had not yet been added to our townhouse lease. What did they want from me? As far as I knew Adnan was presumably in jail. It had already been ten years. What on earth did I have to offer now? Why bother sending someone across the country to look for little old me? Wait...who were "they?" Was this person really working for the lawyer or was it Adnan or perhaps someone else? Was this person going to report back to whoever their employer was with my information, if they were able to confirm my location? Was I in danger? Like I said before, I have a very active imagination, so these are just some of the panicking thoughts I had.

"No way. What!? He's still in jail, right?" I said and my husband shrugged his shoulders. The first thing that came to my head was "I'm not here!"

I then told my husband to tell the investigator that he knew me but that I did not indeed live there anymore. I also told him to get her contact information and say that he would get it to me. So like a good husband that's exactly what he did. It wasn't until the investigator got snarky and rude with him (probably because she knew he was lying) did he have more to say. It was at this time that he belted back, "Given what I know about the case, sounds like the guy did it," and shut the door in the investigators face. Never mind that my husband and I actually had no factual knowledge about the case. All my husband knew were things that I had told him. All I knew were rumors that I had heard back in high school. It had been some time since I had even spoken about the tragedy with anyone else. I hardly ever spoke of it in terms of Adnan, rather that it was simply the tragedy of the nice Asian girl who was murdered during my senior year of high school, occasionally adding in the fact that I may have talked to the guy who killed her on the same day he did it. Most people never asked details at that point in the conversation and if they did I would always say something like how crazy it was because he always seemed so nice.

After the encounter with the investigator it's fair to say that I was shaken and a bit in shock. The investigator had left my husband with a business card for defense attorney Justin Brown. After the investigator was gone, I simply sat on the couch staring at Brown's business card for what seemed like ten minutes. As I stared, I began to wonder more and more about the murder that occurred eleven years before. This Justin Brown character had apparently gone through a lot of trouble to track me down. I had lived in three different states since my days at Woodlawn High School. How did the investigator find me? I had not had my own lease since I came to the state in 2005. Since that time, I always had a sublet. I didn't have a criminal past, my Myspace was private and none of my family or friends had been spoken to (to my knowledge). What the hell was going on? *That was ten years ago,* I thought. *Did Adnan do it?* Again I found my head swarming with questions. The more that I thought about it, the more it became clear to me that I was going to need some answers in order to have some peace of mind.

By this time my husband had left the house again and I was alone. The thought of contacting Justin directly stressed me out and seemed like a bad idea. I wasn't very knowledgeable about criminal court or lawyers, but I assumed that Brown would simply try and convince me to do what was right for his client and not what was morally right. Considering that I had been under the assumption that Adnan had received a fair trial, I assumed that Brown was the attorney of a convicted murderer. From a naïve perspective, defense attorneys are supposed to be the people who represent the bad guys. They are thought of as the ones who lie, cheat the system and do whatever is necessary to win their cases. I wasn't so sure I wanted to take my lead from one of the bad guys. Also, as I stated in the SERIAL podcast, the idea of a convicted murderer (his associates, family or friends) knowing where you live is pretty unsettling, so I didn't want to confirm that I actually had been located. Although Adnan's family had never given me any reason to fear them, it was a pretty intense feeling knowing that they had spent a lot of money to send someone to the other side of the country to find me. Blame it on years of watching television and movies, but I feared that my lack of cooperation might not be received too well by whoever was stuck with that bill. I had not made my final decision on the matter but I did decide that I needed to do a little more homework before volunteering to get involved all willy-nilly.

First thing I did was I take to the Internet. First I looked up Justin Brown and checked out his credentials. I then made a phone call to my Washington cousin-in-law who works as an attorney to ask him questions. He was working, but I spoke to his wife and she said that unfortunately with me living in Oregon, I was at a loss for accurate legal advice. I was told that I should contact a Maryland attorney. Makes sense, right? Knowing that our income was limited at the time and that I could not afford to retain an attorney, I then called my grandfather to see if he knew of a lawyer that would answer my questions "pro bono." As par for the course I got the attorney's voicemail and was left back at square one, still clueless as ever and feeling more panicked by the minute. That's when I got the idea to look up the original case prosecutor. I figured if anyone would give me the truth and not mislead me, it would be that person, aka "The Good Guy." After all, Urick was there at the trial, right?! I then skimmed through an old online news article about the case, and that's when I came across the name Kevin Urick. At that point I did an Internet search for Kevin Urick in Maryland and found several numbers that seemed promising. Luckily for me it only took a few tries and I was on the phone with Urick in no time.

The Kevin Urick Call

When I called Kevin Urick, I was immediately taken aback because he answered the phone (not a secretary). I knew that he would most likely not know who I was. It had been ten years since the trial and considering that I was never involved with it, there would be no way for him to recognize my name. That being my assumption, I introduced myself and told him about seeing Adnan Syed in the Woodlawn Public Library on January 13th, 1999. I told him that I was concerned because an investigator had just shown up at my house in Oregon and the visit had raised some concerns. I told him that I had signed a statement in reference to January 13th back in 2000 and wanted to know if he had any idea what was going on currently with the case. I also wanted his professional opinion on what the ramifications of signing the document in 2000 might be. I wanted to know if he was familiar with the type of document and if I could be subpoenaed because of it. I explained to him that at the time of writing the statement I was only seventeen and wanted to know if that statement might have anything to do with Mr. Brown's reasoning for reaching out to me now. It's at that moment that Mr. Urick placed me on a brief hold in order to "check his computer system" as he put it.

After waiting for what seemed like less than a minute Mr. Urick informed me that there were no open cases for Adnan Syed. He said that there was nothing that he could see from his end. It was at this point that he put great emphasis on the fact that normally he wouldn't talk to someone like me but that legally it was okay because he was no longer the prosecutor handling the Syed case. Hearing that felt great to me, because it was at that very moment that I assumed I was about to be stone-walled. I didn't know that when I called Urick, he was no longer tied to the Syed case. I naturally assumed he would direct me to obtaining my own attorney just like everyone else had. To hear that he was no longer the prosecutor and that he was actually about to open up about it was both a tremendous surprise and a relief.

Now, I am aware of the controversy surrounding this conversation with Kevin Urick. I am aware that I have been accused of recanting the story behind my original affidavit. I'm also aware of the testimony that Mr. Urick gave in which he stated I informed him of being pressured by the Syed family. I cannot recall every exact word that came out of my mouth during my conversation with Mr. Urick but what I can tell you is what I testified to is true. I don't know what that man thinks he heard or if he has other motivations for testifying the way he did. All I can attest to is the intent of my call, what was told to me in response and what that response heavily influenced me to do. I'm not here to play he said, she said. You can look at the information yourself and come to your own rational conclusions. If any legal reprimands come his way as a result, they're not coming from me. I think having everyone know the entire story and seeing the evidence of what I was told is satisfying enough for me.

In any case, my intentions for calling him were pretty simple and straightforward. They were never to recant my affidavit or my letters to Adnan. My intentions were never to inform him that the Syed family pressured me into doing anything. If you've made that assumption based on Urick's 2010 testimony, I'd have to say you've been duped. I recently asked my attorney how the hell he was even allowed to testify to that "nonsense" as I put it. To me it would seem like hearsay. Unfortunately, as it was explained to me, a post-conviction hearing is very different from a trial. There is a lot more leeway given to both parties and most of what is typically discussed in those hearings tends to be a lot of hearsay. Makes no sense to me but it is what it is, I suppose. In any case the remainder of my conversation with Kevin Urick was also pretty simple and straightforward. Urick told me that since he didn't see any open cases for Syed, that most likely his lawyer was preparing to file an appeal. He said since Mr. Syed was serving a life sentence and because of the fact that the conviction had almost reached ten years of age they were probably trying to put a last effort together to appeal before May 10th of that year. Urick also said that, most likely, the defense was getting close to exhausting all of their appeals and that they were probably trying to use me in conjunction with other things, as an effort to get a final appeal. This intrigued me and considering that he was giving me straightforward answers, my questions began to flow. Unfortunately for me this next part is a little fuzzy only because I don't remember if it was I that brought up Cristina Gutierrez or if it was Kevin Urick. Nevertheless, Urick told me that Justin Brown was full of bullshit if his claim was that Cristina Gutierrez was incompetent due to her health issues. He told me that she was one of the best lawyers in Maryland and that anything alluding to her incompetence was nonsense. Being that, at the time, I had no knowledge of Gutierrez's multiple sclerosis or her disbarment, I completely believed Urick. I mean after all it sounds reasonable that a defense lawyer would do and say anything to get his client out of prison, right? I then told Urick that I had not followed the original trial and asked him what happened. I specifically asked him about what led to Syed's conviction. Urick then happily began to discuss the details of the trial to me. Urick told me that Adnan's fingerprints were in Hae's car and there was DNA recovered at the crime scene (which I was not asked about during my testimony because it wasn't written in my "Urick Notes"). That later pissed me off in 2015 because I came to find out that it was Adnan's palm print on an atlas in the car and not just general fingerprints everywhere. Back then we didn't have GPS. Everyone used atlases and it would be no surprise to find Adnan's prints on Hae's atlas. I was also angry because I learned that the DNA collected at the crime scene was never tested. So we have no idea whether it belonged to Adnan or not.

Nevertheless, Urick made everything sound relative to Adnan's guilt. He said that a student named Jay confessed to helping bury Hae's body in Leakin Park. He said that Jay testified in court and that Urick himself had presented cell phone records that placed the two boys in Leakin Park during the very time that the burial occurred. As you can imagine I was wowed by all this information. Along the way I had heard that Jay Wilds was involved somehow back at the time of Adnan's arrest. I didn't know he was actually a witness to the crime or that he was involved in the trial. Being that Jay was my upperclassman and not someone that I personally liked, I never had a reason to speak to him. I think I only have one memory of Jay and I'm not even sure about it because, once again, nobody else remembers the day in question.

In any case, Urick continued to talk and I continued to listen and take notes. He told me about how quickly it took to convict Mr. Syed and he even said, "If I [myself] had any doubt that he [Syed] killed Hae [Min Lee] then it would be my moral obligation to see that he [Syed] didn't serve any time." Just then my husband came up stairs and began to speak. I shooed him away and continued listening to Urick. As I listened and agreed with his previous sentiment he scoffed and also said, "Oh, he killed that girl, there is no doubt in my mind!" I found the statement so profound that I wrote it in quotes. Just the way he said "Oh" as you would when talking about something blatantly obvious. I found this to be very convincing. As if his previous statement wasn't good enough he followed it by saying, "Yeah, there's a snowball's chance in hell that they [Justin Brown] could reopen the case with those type of accusations. Let alone get him [Syed] off!"

As I think about this case now, that quote makes me chuckle a little. Isn't it ironic? As if there was anything more to say Urick told me one more time that the defense was wasting the court's time. He said that at the trial, the defense had a list of about eighty individuals that were willing to lie and place Adnan at the mosque. Urick said that he knew these people to be liars because every single last one of them backed down once the state produced the cell phone records showing that Adnan was in Leakin Park. As I sat there listening to what Urick was telling me, I shook my head in disbelief. *How awful and what a shame,* I thought.

As we ended the conversation, Urick gave me one final thought to chew on (which again I was not asked about during my testimony because it wasn't written in my "Urick Notes"). He reminded me of the fact that the defense already had my original affidavit in their possession. The defense already knew my testimony and could use the affidavit in court if they needed to. He reminded me that I had not received a subpoena, so in essence I was free to do whatever I wanted. I agreed and we ended our thirty-four-minute phone call. To say the least, I was sold on Adnan's guilt. I was sold on Justin Brown's intentions to manipulate and exploit loopholes in our criminal justice system. To me I had received the case facts straight from the horse's mouth. The prosecutor, the good guy, had shelled out everything I needed to hear. I decided not to call Justin Brown. In fact, I didn't even keep his business card.

CHAPTER FOUR

MAKING OF A PODCAST

Normally I don't think I would have ever agreed to have my voice on the SERIAL podcast. Not because I regret talking with Sarah Koenig. My reasoning is a little vainer than I'm happy to admit. As horrible as it sounds, I absolutely hate the way my voice sounds when recorded. There's only one reason that I agreed to speak with Sarah Koenig on the phone in 2014 and it wasn't because I wanted to "get famous." I don't think anyone anticipated SERIAL's success, most of all Sarah Koenig. In fact, the reason that I agreed to help was quite the opposite. Unbeknownst to Sarah, I wanted nothing more than to be left alone at the time she reached out to me. I've never told anyone other than my husband this story before, but Sarah actually found my home address.

There it was, four years after the private detective showed

up at our last residence and we were now living in Washington state. My husband and I had literally moved on from the event and were enjoying our new life as parents. Out of the blue one day came a letter in our mailbox. The letter was from Sarah Koenig, a reporter from *This American Life* and she explained that she was doing a "story" about Adnan's Syed trial in 2000. She stated in the letter that she had a great interest in speaking with me and left her contact information for me to touch base with her. Now as you can imagine after receiving this letter, I became stressed. Although this written request was not as invasive as the private detective four years prior, it still did not sit well with me. Once again I was jarred by the fact that yet again another stranger had tracked me down, in yet another state. After the event in 2010 I did some digging and eventually determined the previous private investigator had located my husband and I through our home business. In 2010, I wasn't aware that I was a person of interest to anyone and as a result I had my home address listed as my business address. Little did I know that anyone with half a brain and a lot of determination to find me could locate me simply by checking the Secretary of State's office, where our LLC information was on file. Upon moving to Washington state a few months later my husband and I decided that going forward, it would be a wiser idea to use a post office box for our business address. Nevertheless, here I was walking to my house with a letter in my hand from an overzealous investigative reporter. Shortly after her letter Sarah also managed to reach me through my business email address. I wasn't very surprised because my company website is easily accessible. Her persistence was more annoying than anything. Based on what Urick had explained to me in 2010, I was still under the impression that the State of Maryland had overwhelming evidence to convict Adnan back in 2000. As far as I was aware, Adnan Syed had been rightfully convicted of the murder of Hae Min Lee. Now fourteen years into his life sentence and having exhausted all his appeals, it seemed strange to me that any investigation into his conviction was even a thing of interest to anyone. Since I had never been subpoenaed by Justin Brown (that I was aware of) and my affidavit was on file, I couldn't imagine why this woman (Sarah) now also wanted to speak to me. She had no personal attachments to the defendant, nor was she a member of the court. I couldn't imagine what more I could possibly offer her that she didn't already know.

I was curious about the full nature of her request, but I was all too familiar with the concept of curiosity killing the cat. I didn't want to confirm to her that she had found my home address. I worried that if I didn't call her back that she would show up at my front door, too. According to Jay Wilds's interview in the Intercept, that was probably a smart assumption on my part, as she did travel across country to track him down. At the time, that was something that I could only speculate happening, but it was definitely something that I did not want to transpire. In the end, I decided that because I did live so far away, I would put the letter aside and give my actions some further thought before proceeding. I tucked the letter away in my underwear drawer and proceeded to go about my normal stay-at-home mom life. Unfortunately, I soon became preoccupied with other things and after a few days had forgotten about the letter entirely. Then as I stated before, one day I was checking my company email and once again I had a message from Sarah Koenig. The message said:

Hello Mrs. Chapman, I'm the producer from the radio show This American Life. I just wanted to verify that you got my letter in the mail? Did you receive it? If not, I'd be happy to send it again, or just email it if that's easier.

Thanks very much, Sarah K. xxx-xxx-xxxx

Once again I found myself facing the perseverance of another third party investigator wanting to speak to me. As I stated before, I've actually been stalked, so the feeling of being "found" is very unsettling to me. There is nothing like minding your own business when you receive a phone call one Saturday morning and someone says, "Hi Asia, don't you want to know how I found you?" To me, a private detective at my door, a letter sent to my home and now an email sent to my business was just plain annoying and invasive.

In hindsight I know for a fact that Sarah never meant

any harm, however at the time all I could think of was telling her to "go kick rocks." In the end, I conceded to both emailing and calling Sarah that next day. Little did I know, that was the start of a small kinship between us. At the time, I had no idea what type of person Sarah Koenig was and whether she could be trusted. Now I have a better understanding of the caliber of character and journalistic integrity she has. In the beginning when Sarah and I first talked, I thought nothing much about her actual "story." When I first picked up the phone to call her, I had no idea what I was stepping into. Neither did Sarah.

In our conversation that followed it began to feel like one amateur sleuth bringing another up to speed. Like I said before, when Sarah first reached out to me, I was very suspicious of who she was, her affiliation to the case and her motives for even investigating it to begin with. I wanted to know who had hired her, how she knew about the case and if she was acting as an advocate for Adnan Syed. As we began to chat more, it became clear to me that she was in fact very impartial about the case. Although she was a reporter, at the time she was no Barbara Walters-type celebrity reporter (like she is now) and she didn't seem to have a dog in the fight.

As I began to talk more with her, I saw that her only motivation was to find out the truth and report on the facts. Of course those goals had their own motivations, but who can blame a girl for wanting to be successful at what she does? I saw Sarah as a truth seeker and in that sense she reminded me a lot of myself. It became apparent to me that she had started off not knowing anything about the case and trial. All she initially knew was the fact that Hae was murdered, Adnan was in jail for Hae's murder and that I might be an alibi. Although Rabia was the person whom introduced her to the case, it was abundantly clear to me that Rabia nor anyone associated with Adnan's defense team was "running the show." After fifteen years of having this situation randomly making cameos in my life, I decided to talk to Sarah. I liked Sarah's position on the matter and I figured that it was "safe" to open up to her. Little did I know, that was the very moment in which things began to get more complicated in my life.

The Interview

The day I called Sarah was a normal day with the exception that I had been bitching to my husband about Sarah's correspondence. After some time, I was still indecisive on whether I should call her. In any case, that particular day I guess my husband had heard enough. Let me just say, God bless my husband because he always gives me his opinion straight. "Go see what the hell she wants!" he said. "They're obviously not going to leave you alone, unless you tell them to! If you don't want to talk, tell them that and be done!" In that moment I knew everything that he was saying was right. Part of me knew I needed to talk to somebody about it. Why not her? I guess that's why I picked up the phone and gave Sarah a call. When I called Sarah, I made sure to use my star-six-seven feature on my phone. I wasn't about to relinquish my personal contact information to some random nosy stranger. Sarah answered the phone and on the fly I concocted a story and lied about how I had not received her physical letter but instead was reaching out to her because of her email. Thinking about it now, I laugh because I could tell by her response that she didn't whole-heartedly believe my lie. Now I chuckle whenever I listen to SERIAL and hear Sarah's recollection of that first conversation. The same disbelieving and confused sentiment comes across in her tone in the podcast. I admit now that it was a dumb lie to tell, but at the time I didn't trust the idea of confirming my address to her. As I began to speak with Sarah, she explained that she was a reporter for *This American Life* and that someone vested in the Syed case had brought this story to her attention. She explained that upon checking out the case, she became highly intrigued and decided to do her own "story" about the case facts. She also explained that she was in the process of speaking to multiple people from my high school and that I was an important person of particular interest.

Immediately I liked the fact that her story didn't seem to center around me. It soon became clear to me that she was not only a reporter but also a fairly impartial one in her pursuit for the truth. I soon began to see that she was interested in both

Hae's murder and Adnan's conviction. She explained that she had been doing tons of research on the old case files and had become completely baffled on how the trial transpired the way it did. She told me details of the case that I had never known before and I began to agree that something didn't seem right. She asked about my letters to Adnan and my affidavit, and as we talked, a kinship began to form. As a result, I began to lower my guard and realize that perhaps this was the right person to finally tell my story to.

Looking back, I don't regret talking to Sarah Koenig at all, however I do wish that perhaps I had taken an extra day or two in order to research her professional affiliations. Perhaps then, I would have realized that I was engaging in an interview with a podcast reporter and that the actual audio of our interview would be aired all over the world. At the time I didn't even know what a podcast was. Had I'd known what it was, that information most definitely would have influenced my decision and determined to what capacity I chose to participate. For instance, I would have answered her questions more precisely, more thoroughly and less off-the-cuff. I would have spoken more clearly as to compensate for the poor audio quality and I would have most definitely been more aware of my cadence. I would have not used so many similes and generalizations when recalling memories from January 13th, 1999. Sarah was the first to ask me my opinions and the first to not be affiliated with a side. I didn't realize at the time that my interview was going out to the masses, but I definitely wouldn't take it back now for the world. The way everything has happened is indeed pretty crazy but I believe it has all played out the way God intended. From that day in the library on, there have been so many serendipitous occurrences that only can be explained as fate; everything from Derrick being late, to Gutierrez being disbarred, to SERIAL and more. If nothing else I am thankful for SERIAL, because it brought out a lot of things that would have otherwise forever gone unnoticed.

Three weeks had gone by since my interview with Sarah. We had stayed in contact over that time, but it was minimal. Specifically, our conversations had been limited to helping her track down other people of interest. The third week of February hit and all of the sudden Sarah had started to complain about the sound quality of my recorded interview. Initially I didn't think much of it because the fact that Sarah was a podcast journalist had been completely missed by me. The fact that *This American Life* was an affiliate of National Public Radio had also skipped my radar (I know—dumb). I had never listened to National Public Radio or *This American Life*. At that point in my life I was adjusting to life with a two-year-old and an eight-month-old; I was living in a "mommy bubble."

When Sarah said the audio was crummy, I assumed that she was having trouble making out some information for her written article. Finally, one day Sarah asked if she could rerecord my interview and not thinking, I obliged. It wasn't until later that I began to get suspicious of her intentions. If she were merely doing a "story," why was she stressing the audio quality issue so much? Her persistence started to throw up red flags in my mind; *I thought the audio was just for notation purposes. Why doesn't she just ask me to paraphrase the crappy audio for her? Can I really trust her? Is she really who she says she is?*

Incidentally, all of these questions could have been easily been answered by a simple phone call but instead I chose to stay silent. Eventually the day came to rerecord my interview with Sarah in a sound studio. The only problem was that morning I found out that my husband had scheduled me for an important gastroenterologist appointment. I also found out that he had forgotten to tell me about it (got to love husbands, right?). Unable to reschedule the appointment with the doctor, I was forced to call Sarah and reschedule with her. Unfortunately for both Sarah and myself, I also took that coincidence as a "sign" and never rescheduled a time to rerecord. In the days that followed Sarah reached out to me several times, but I ignored her. I had told myself that something was off with her and at the time I thought it best to cut my losses and move on. The unfortunate part was that ignoring Sarah left her with many unanswered follow-up questions that I never paid any attention to. It wasn't until after SERIAL came out that I was even aware of what those question would have been. Some of those questions were as follows:

Why were you so worried when the PI came to your house?

Why were you reluctant to talk to Justin Brown?

Did you call Kevin Urick?

Was it true what Kevin Urick said at the post-conviction hearing in 2010?

Are you sure that your memory of speaking to Adnan in the library is tied to literal snow?

Talk about kicking myself in the ass! If only I had asked Sarah about the audio recording. If only I had realized it was for "radio," like she had stated in her email. If only I had entertained her offer to rerecord knowing that it was for more than her notation purposes. I could have thoroughly, clearly and concisely answered her questions and none of these crazy theories about my accuracy or motivations would even exist!

Finding Out About SERIAL

When SERIAL came out it was like someone dropped a bomb in my lap. It hit the airwaves and instantly became true crime crack for the masses. It had already been available one whole day by the time I found out about it. By then I was late to the party. The day it came screaming into my life, I was home alone with the kids. Out of the blue I started getting Facebook messages, texts and emails from friends across the country saying that I "was on the radio." I knew I indeed had not been on the radio, let alone anything that would be nationwide, so I chalked it up to a case of mistaken identity. Then a close friend told me, "It's you! I'm literally listening to your voice, right now, as we speak!" Then another friend said, "No...Internet radio. You're on the radio on the Internet." Instantly I was bewildered and excited. I had no clue until someone said "It's about Adnan and Hae" and my stomach dropped. I panicked. I could feel my blood boiling. That Sarah Koenig had posted my interview! I knew she was up to no good! I immediately dropped everything and headed over to the serialpodcast.org website and there in big bold letters I saw the words "THE ALIBI" and I was mortified. As I hit play and began to listen my anger and anxiety began to grow. By the time I finished the first episode I was pacing around the house having a full-fledged shit-fit. "How could she have done this to me, I trusted her?!" I thought. "What a bitch!"

To this day, I have no idea how on earth I even made it through that episode without having a heart attack. I finished listening to episode one; all the while my phone kept blowing up with message notifications from friends. By the time I stopped listening the only thought I could muster was: *I need to call my husband and I need to call him right now!* Of course when I called Phillip I was in a state of frenzy. Between shouting out words like "interview," "recording," and "the Internet" I'm sure he thought I had lost my marbles. Finally, he yelled for me to calm down and start at the beginning. I reminded him of my call with Sarah Koenig earlier in the year and then I told him about SERIAL. Being the cool cucumber that he is, he told me to chill out, not to worry about it and that it would all eventually go away. I wanted to believe him, but I had this horrible feeling that it wouldn't. As a matter of fact, I knew it wouldn't because I was already hooked and wanted to listen to episode two.

After listening to episode two, I became so distraught. I decided that I didn't have the intestinal fortitude to listen to anymore. Within the next two weeks I started hearing more and more about SERIAL. It was literally everywhere! As it grew, so did my stress level. After weeks of nicely suggesting to Phillip that he check it out with me, I started hinting to him that it was getting more popular. Every time I brought it up he downplayed my concern until finally one day I snapped and said, "*No!* You don't understand! This shit is everywhere! You *need* to listen to this shit with me *right now!*" It sounded something like that scene from *I'm Gonna Git You Sucka.* You know, the one where Dawnn Lewis turns all exorcist and says she's got cramps. If you don't know what I'm talking about go Google it right now. I guarantee you it's on YouTube and that you will find it hilarious.

In any case, with that one comment he knew I wasn't messing around. We immediately sat down went to www.serial-podcast.org and pressed play (for episode one). At the end of the episode, I looked at him and the look on his face literally read "Holy shit!" "Play the next one," he said with a menacing grin on his face. After that we spent the remainder of the day and late into the night (eight hours straight) listening to the entire podcast—everything except the final episode, which had not come out yet. Don't ask me where my children were or what the hell they were doing during that time. We had been consumed by SERIAL.

After listening to the entire podcast, let's just say I was not too happy with Sarah. Okay, scratch that. I was livid. I was mad about the content layout and the jokes at my expense. I was mad about its popularity and I blamed it all on Sarah Koenig. I blamed Sarah for unethically using my audio in the podcast. I blamed her for making me the lynchpin in the story. I yelled at her for making me sound like the bad guy, the villain. I even yelled at her for making my husband sound like a giant asshole (his words, not mine). Oh, I let her have it good!

Now, I have to give credit where credit is due. Sarah kept her cool with me when I was being far less than friendly. Let's just say she sternly put me in my place and reminded me of all the subtle details that I had overlooked: radio, NPR, *This American Life*, record in a sound studio for better audio quality. She reminded me that at any time I could have clarified things with her, but instead that I had decided to cease and desist all communications back in February. I had to give it to her. She was 100 percent correct. The breakdown in communication had been all my fault. The misconception of her intentions had been all my fault, so I apologized (many times). She forgave my anger, we chalked it up to semantics and it being a really bad misunderstanding and we moved on.

CHAPTER FIVE

THE RECOMMITMENT

When I spoke to Sarah Koenig in early 2014, I was told that Adnan's legal team was under the impression that I was a hostile witness. I was told that the court's decision was primarily based on Urick's testimony, my husband's comment to the investigator and my inability to appear in court. I was told that the Syed defense team was afraid that any further contact would come off as pressuring, especially since the prosecution was already accusing the Syed family of doing so before.

In their defense, I can completely understand why they thought that. Thanks to Urick I was under the impression that they were an exploitative group who would do anything to get an appeal. Because of Kevin Urick I saw Adnan as being 100 percent guilty and deserving of a lengthy prison stay. I didn't want to contribute to some sleazy underhanded attempt to get a convicted murderer out of prison. However, when my husband and I listened to the Serial Podcast, we were both sickened. Although neither of us can make heads or tails of Adnan's guilt, we both agreed that the podcast made it seem Adnan had not received a fair trial, especially considering that I had never been presented before the court. It made me sick to my stomach to know that a conversation with me had been discussed without my knowledge or consent, that a falsehood had been seen as fact. Not to mention the idea of that falsehood being used as the basis for denying Adnan's appeal. Hell, anyone's appeal. We instantly both agreed that we needed to make ourselves available to do whatever was needed to set the wrong right. Unfortunately, doing so was slightly more complicated than we anticipated.

Nightmares

When involved in a situation like this case, one expects a considerable amount of stress and tension. What you don't expect are highly vivid nightmares. My best bet this that the contemplation of this case seeped so far into my brain that it had an equally strong hold on my subconscious mind. Unlike the conscious mind, there's not really much anyone can do to control or stop those thoughts (besides waking up of course). I think it's why these thoughts are often the most terrifying. In order to tell you about a time that shook me to my core, I'll have to jump ahead a little bit.

The night of January 12th was a normal night by most

standards. My husband and I had made dinner, gave our children a bath, read them a story and tucked them in for bed. After that, I took to spending quality time with my husband, while we watched a couple of our favorite television shows. The only thing outside of the norm that night was that I had also been working on finishing my final copy of my 2015 affidavit. After adding and editing its contents once again, I began to get sleepy. Curious about the time, I checked my phone and to my surprise it was past midnight. It was officially January 13th. "Great," I thought. "Now I have to edit the stinkin' date again." So I flipped to the final page of my affidavit and proceeded to change the document date.

All of a sudden it dawned on me and I felt terrible. It was January 13th, the sixteen-year anniversary of the disappearance of Hae Min Lee. I remember feeling sad and noted how ironic it was for me to be finishing my affidavit on that very day. In any case, I finished up my affidavit, emailed it and took myself to bed. Unbeknownst to me as I lay in bed feeling drowsy, my husband had also fallen asleep, but on the couch. Soon after falling asleep myself, I felt my duvet cover slip away from the right side of my body. By that time, I assumed that my husband had made his way to bed and was once again stealing the covers (as he often does). In any right, I didn't pay it much mind.

Slowly I felt the temperature change in my bedroom. Coupled with having no bed covering on me, the temperature change was only slightly noticeable enough that it lightly roused me from my sleep. Half awake, I lay there and became more and more aware of my body's own presence. I could feel myself lying flat on my back and feeling an enormous weight holding me down. I then realized that I could see around my bedroom and therefore assumed that I was no longer asleep. I looked up towards my bedroom ceiling fan and there I saw a sight that felt like it made my hair turn white. There, floating in midair, about four feet directly above me, was Hae Min Lee. Absolutely scared shitless I tried even harder to move my body but could not. I was literally frozen into place. As I felt my heart pounding in my chest and my breath shortening, it became completely evident to me that I was having a full-fledged panic attack. Unable to do anything else, I stared at the apparition, wide-eyed and full of fear. As I looked up at her I began to notice that she looked exactly as I remembered her in high school and that she was floating in an odd manner. She was adorned with a long white dress that appeared to be gently drifting in an abyss of invisible water. You could tell that her skin was ceramic china white, however there was an overall shade of light blue to her skin and dress. Her hair was black as onyx and her eyes dark as coal.

As I continued to stare at her, she reached out her hand to me. Being that I was restrained and full of fright, we were unable to touch. I noticed a sort of sadness about her, as if she was not at rest. In that moment I sensed that she was trying to speak to me, but no words left her mouth. It felt as if she were trying to tell me something, but could not. I don't know how I know this, but it felt as if she was trying to tell me who killed her. As my emotions and adrenaline continued to run high, my body went into supreme panic attack mode. Just when I thought my heart would explode, I suddenly broke the confines of my supernatural restraints and jolted myself back into what I can only perceive as reality. Hae was gone and nothing except my overhead ceiling fan remained turning. I immediately went to reach for my husband, only to realize that he had indeed fallen asleep on the couch. Feeling some comfort in the fact that I was alone, I settled back into a calmer mood. Nevertheless, I was unable to return back to sleep for several hours. To this day, I'm not sure if I was dreaming or not. To this day I can't shake the feeling that I may have seen my first and only ghost.

Who Helped and Who Didn't

After I heard Kevin Urick's post-conviction testimony on the podcast I knew immediately that I needed to reach out to someone. The problem was once again that I was unsure of whom. Both Sarah Koenig and Justin Brown were possibly good starts, however I was extremely concerned with what to say to either one of them. By this time, it was December of 2014; the podcast was wrapping up. It was only days away from airing its final episode. On a whim, I decided it best to randomly call Sarah from my blocked cell number (as I am now famous for doing).

I tend to call Sarah this way a lot, as she will tell you. I don't know, is that paranoid or smart?

It's weird now to think that my first instinct was to call Sarah. I don't know her well enough to consider her a friend, but I do consider us to have a weird kinship. Hearing Urick's testimony made me feel sucker-punched and bewildered. My opinion was that it was bullshit, my husband's opinion was also that it was bullshit and I just wanted to reach out to someone else who would also would see it as bullshit. For whatever reason, I felt like Sarah was that person at the time.

During the call, I could tell that Sarah wanted to know my thoughts about Urick's testimony, specifically, if I thought Urick had been in violation of prosecutorial misconduct. I told her my thoughts and naturally she wanted to know if she could include this new development in the final episode of SERIAL. I wasn't comfortable with that, so I asked her to first let me seek out an attorney for advice on the matter. I tried over a two-day period to seek legal advice on the matter but it was to no avail. Once again no west coast attorney could advise me on the ins and outs of Maryland law and no Maryland attorney would even call me back. Just trying to explain the situation to an attorney felt trivial and silly. There was such an extensive back-story that needed to be told every time. As the days passed I got even more desperate. I once again tried reaching out to my grandfather's attorney, but the advice that I got from his assistant (mind you)

was neither reassuring nor was it in the vicinity of being relevant to my situation. I can only assume it's because they weren't
familiar with the case (at all) and were not familiar with the
podcast at the time.

As you can imagine, I was pretty irritable and stressed
about what I should do at that point. Aside from Phillip, I didn't
feel like anyone truly had my back. I felt alone and I wanted
to get the truth out to both the court and the public. I was unsure of the best course of action and had no one to advise me
other than an overzealous journalist. That's not meant to be a
dig toward Sarah at all. I like Sarah, but at the end of the day
let's keep it real. She's a professional journalist and SERIAL
is her brainchild. I'm not a lawyer and things were already
like a geyser beyond my control. I didn't want to make matters
worse by doing something stupid, once again. My inability to
find legal advice back in 2010 was the primary reason I was
in this predicament with Sarah. The thought of repeating the
same mistake was causing me to become even more paranoid. I
worried about the effects of exposing myself directly to the prosecution, the defense and the public. I later contacted Sarah back
and it was becoming apparent that she really wanted to include
"the update" in the final episode of the SERIAL podcast. She
was very polite and respectful with her request, but I could tell
that she was chomping at the bit to get my approval. I wanted
to throw caution to the wind and say screw it, but something

just wouldn't settle in my spirit. I just couldn't get comfortable with the idea of granting her full authority like that. I therefore declined her offer to address my feelings in the last episode of the podcast. I did however grant her permission to say that we had recently spoken and that I was continuing to stick by my original affidavit.

After the final episode, my lack of legal representation once again came up in conversation. Sarah came through with the save and offered to help me locate an attorney. After much consideration, I gave Sarah my authorization. I inquired about the attorney's affiliation to the SERIAL team and allowed Sarah to set up a time for me to call the attorney. When the time came, I once again blocked my cell number and proceeded to call. By the time my call connected, I received the office's voicemail because unbeknownst to me, Larry (the attorney) was on the other line. I left a message and emailed Sarah about this unfortunate turn of events. She immediately offered up another attorney's contact info. By the time she did so, I was already back on the phone with Larry (the first attorney).

During my conversation with Larry, I found out two things. Number one: Larry was not offering to work pro bono (free). Number two: Larry was not cheap. I was advised not to speak to any media and learned that Larry's services would require a $1,500 retainer along with ongoing hourly rates. "Holy shit!" I thought. "I'm not the one on trial for murder." This understandably floored me. Call me naive but I could not fathom paying that kind of money when I was not the one accused of committing a crime. The idea of shelling out that kind of dough on an attorney would have meant some significant budgetary constraints on my family. It also seemed ludicrous that I would need to incur such a heavy cost in order to receive legal advice, for merely stepping up to do the right thing. Before my conversation ended with Larry, I was already over Larry and feared that I would now be entering the media circus alone. Of course I had not seen Sarah's other message, so I had not realized that Sarah had already recommended another attorney.

Not knowing that this was the case, I had already conceded to going into the situation unprotected. I picked up my phone, once again blocked my number and called Justin Brown. It took less than one minute for Justin to advise me to seek my own counsel. He was polite about it. I knew that it wasn't so much that he didn't care about me; rather he cared about protecting his client and his case. I knew that I was not his priority and therefore could not expect him to have my best interest at heart. Sounds messed up, but it's the truth. I told Justin about my conversation with the attorney and he responded by telling me that Larry was one of the best lawyers in the state. I laughed because while Justin spoke about Larry's talent, all I could recall was the "screw you, pay me" attitude that I had received from Larry on the phone call.

Coincidentally during my call with Justin, I noticed Sarah's message about the second attorney. It was about a guy named Gary Proctor. However serendipitous, Justin mentioned that he was familiar with Gary's work—that he was a good attorney and perhaps he would do the work for less than Larry. I ended my call with Justin and immediately proceeded to call the man who would soon become my saving grace, Gary Proctor.

The first time I talked to Gary, I knew that he was the right attorney for me. He's extremely funny, easy to talk to and down to earth. He doesn't over complicate things and he gives you his advice straight. I was told before speaking with him that Gary is a "true Irishman" and as such has a pretty candid personality and sense of humor. In any case, I like Gary's personality. If we lived closer to one another, I could see my husband and I having dinner with Gary and his wife pretty often.

After speaking with me Gary got on the phone and received a case update from Justin Brown. Gary then introduced me to another associate that he works with named Ali and we began laying a strategy down for my recommitment to disseminating the truth. Gary basically told me that he was there for my benefit, that he had my back. He said that I could participate as much or little as I wanted, or not at all. He explained that he had no allegiance to any party other than mine. Before the call ended Gary stressed the importance of our client/attorney

privilege. We discussed his retainer cost and fees. We also discussed me staying above the social media buzz surrounding the
podcast and case and what to do if anyone tried to reach out to
me directly. All in all, it felt extremely comforting to know that I
had my own personal "pit bull" attorney in the event that things
were about to get complicated. It took no time at all for me to
feel comfortable with providing Gary my contact information.
Ironically Gary had no desire to know my current last name or
home address. He said it wasn't currently important and that
we could address "that stuff" if it ever became important. The
best thing about Gary is that he's cool with me texting him. Gary
lets me text him with questions and he responds in turn. We
text each other jokes and new case developments, along with
everything else under the sun. I've texted Gary pictures of my
kids playing and occasionally he will text me just to "check in." I
now know Gary well enough to consider him a friend in addition
to my attorney.

Sometimes I text Gary something and he doesn't text me
back. That usually means something within itself. During those
times I find that most often if I'm asking something stupid,
he will ignore me. I know this because I usually already know
Gary's position and my question is pretty asinine. I've only had
a lawyer maybe two times in my life. Once was for a discrimination lawsuit. The other was when I purchased my home through

private sale. Neither time did I ever get to know the attorneys as anything more than hired hands. This time around with Gary Proctor, things have been quite different. If you're talking about an amazing attorney, you must be talking about Gary Proctor.

CHAPTER SIX

THE CHALLENGE

People always question why it is that I made the decision
to "lawyer up" when I got re-involved in this case. My response
has always been: how could I not? Challenging the word and
testimony of a successful state's attorney is not something that I
take lightly. It's actually something that took me a lot of courage
to do. I've never been in trouble with the law, so the idea of being
on the wrong side of it (in any sense) is very concerning to me.
I'm a middle class, stay-at-home mom who loves her life, pays
her taxes and until lately, never really questioned whether if
those who defend the law are the good guys. So when faced with
a situation in which I was starting to believe that one of our
civil servants may not have done things on the up and up, I was
pretty stunned. I take full responsibility for my stupidity. My
preconceived notion that all prosecutors were the good guys was

foolish and unseasoned. To find out that Urick wasn't the man in the white hat (as Olivia Pope would say) was a hard truth to digest. Not only that, but feeling as if my reputation had been served up on the courtroom floor in exchange for professional bragging rights made me livid.

It's a funny thing to find out through the grapevine that another person has misspoken about your words and intentions. It's another thing to find out through a podcast simultaneously with millions of other people. From the moment that I heard Urick's post-conviction hearing testimony I instantaneously felt like I had been taken advantage of. In my entire life I can't recall ever having felt so duped and foolish. Of course I wrote my second affidavit as an attempt to correct what I saw as a miscarriage of justice, however the contents of that affidavit was also my opportunity to speak out about the miscarriage of trust that I felt I had experienced with Kevin Urick. I wrote my affidavit with pride because I had hoped that others would read it and know, at last, my version of what happened. Some people find it pretty convenient that I say he misinterpreted or misrepresented the contents of our conversation, as to say that I'm now lying about it. I say to those people that it's pretty convenient that Urick didn't testify with his version of our conversation until six months after he influenced me not to participate with Justin Brown. Six months is a pretty substantial amount of time. I bet six months was plenty of time for Urick to feel comfortable with the idea that I wasn't going to participate in the hearing at all. After all, by then I was assumed to have been a hostile witness.

If I truly felt as Urick said I did, wouldn't it have been better for me to tell Justin Brown that myself? If that was the actual conversation that transpired, why didn't Urick just encourage me to call Brown and tell him? How awkward would that have been if I had actually been present at the 2010 post-conviction hearing? Do you think his remarks would have been the same? I seriously doubt it.

That's why I made the decision to release a copy of my affidavit and interview with TheBlaze. The day that my affidavit was made public was a pretty big deal for me. It was one of the best days of this entire experience. Almost as good as testifying at the post-conviction hearing in 2016. For a short time, it felt as if I was using my own voice. It felt like I was both doing the right thing and addressing the man who I felt had violated me in front of the court. I know that when Kevin Urick gave that testimony he had no idea that it would be featured in an internationally-known podcast. However, in life such as in court, that's like saying that a dirt bag who rapes a woman at a public concert has no idea that other people are videotaping it. That, my friends, is the power of God. Proverbs 12:19 says, "Truthful lips endure forever, but a lying tongue lasts only a moment."

When I think about Urick I feel so violated and shameful in the sense that my only faults were being naïve and trusting him when I didn't know where else to turn, allowing my moment of ignorance to be seemingly pitted against me. He opened his vocal coffers to me and seemingly lulled me in with his friendly stature and knowledgeable expertise. He made it feel safe to engage in conversation with him when all the while I was in the midst of what I refer to as the serpent's lair. Normally I pride myself on the lessons that I have learned in life, whether they come easy or hard. In my opinion, this lesson came at a very expensive price. I've learned that the truth can be costly. I feel like not only did Urick rape my integrity when he testified during the first post-conviction hearing, but it is also my opinion that he raped Adnan's civil liberties. I know what real sexual assault victims go through. It's fair to say that a similar sense of violation harbors within me. It makes you feel stupid. It makes you want to hang your head low with shame. It makes you feel used and like you want to ball up and disappear, but it also makes you want to rip off his head and shit down his throat. I figuratively chose the latter.

So what do I personally think about Urick's response to my challenge? Let's review what was said in TheBlaze interview:

"'Absolutely false,' he told TheBlaze. 'I was not the one that brought up anything about evidence. She asked me, was it a strong case? I said yes. That was about the extent of my response.' He said McClain had contacted him because she was concerned about having to testify at Syed's post-conviction hearing. He estimated the call lasted about five minutes. He did not take notes."

Okay, now at first glance this seems like a perfectly acceptable response, but let's dig deeper and ask some questions. Let's play devil's advocate a bit. Say I called Urick and I had questions about my first affidavit. Why didn't Urick refer me to an attorney that could assist me? We already know he's good at that because he helped recommend Jay Wilds an attorney, back during Adnan's trial. Okay, I digress, let's continue.

Assuming Urick is telling the truth, in his own words he stated that I said something to the effect of, "Well, did you have a strong case?" Why, oh, why would I ask him this question with no follow-up question about what made his case so strong? Adnan had been in jail for ten years at this point. Obviously the state had a strong case! Since I had no knowledge of trial facts and evidence it only stands logical to assume that I would ask him for more details! For heaven's sake I didn't even know that Cristina Gutierrez was already dead by 2010! I didn't find that out until four years later when I spoke to Sarah Koenig! Nevertheless, the public is supposed to believe that in the course of a "normal" five-minute conversation, my only question to him was whether or not the state had a strong case. Then he simply answers yes and I'm good with that? I mean, come on! Really? No, no way! You're telling me that you believe a convicted murderer's attorney tracks me down across the country; I search the

Internet, locate the original trial prosecutor, and call him all for a simple "Yes?" Not freakin' likely! Yet, Kevin Urick says that's how it all went down.

At second glance Urick is also quoted as estimating our phone call to have only lasted five minutes. However, when I read that article I immediately found that to be untrue. I mean come on, in what language is a conversation of our magnitude able to be completed within the span of five minutes? The minute I saw that claim I scoffed at it and immediately knew that I had to obtain my Sprint phone records to show otherwise. So on January 21st, 2015, I picked up the phone and called Sprint. To my disappointment Sprint was completely useless. Every time I called, a representative assured me that they were going to have my phone records sent to my home. I even paid a fee to insure that this request was being fulfilled. During my multiple conversations I was told that it would take anywhere from two to five days, and sometimes five to seven days. Contrary to what I was being told, every time I waited patiently nothing arrived. Over the course of the next few weeks, various Sprint representatives informed me of many speculations on why my bills weren't arriving, my favorite being that because I was signed up for e-billing, my phone records were going to my email. Of course I knew this to not be true (no emails from Sprint) so I offered them the opportunity to guess again. No educated guess could be given, so just for kicks I had them change my billing preferences back to physical mail and had the phone records sent out again. Of course, you guessed it, nothing showed up.

On the multiple attempts that followed, I was told to go to Sprint.com and the records would be located there. Unfortunately, that information was also incorrect because you can only see phone records that extend back twenty-four months on their website. Since I had heard this same statement expressed to me many times, I said, "So let me ask you something. When you put that request in to order my records, does that request then go to another department?" After a concerning pause the representative asked me, "What do you mean? I'm sorry, ma'am, I don't understand you."

I responded by repeating myself and saying, "When you put in the request to have my bill printed, where does that request go?" The representative then explained that the request goes to another department. I asked if anyone had contact information for that other department. Of course, you guessed it, he informed me that there was no contact information for that other department. So I then asked Luis (the representative) if he had a direct extension so that when I indeed did not receive my records (as he was promising) I could call him back directly. Luis of course denied me such information. Obviously my conversation with Luis was going nowhere so I ended the call.

Finally, the day of February 11th came. Three weeks had passed and by this time I was good and fed up with Sprint. My last conversation with a Sprint supervisor resulted in him literally promising me that I would be receiving the bills in the mail. Of course nothing showed up. After I decided to make this call, I told myself that I was not going to once again explain the situation to someone low on the Sprint totem pole. Upon starting the conversation, I immediately asked to speak with a Sprint supervisor. The highly poor standard of professionalism and customer service of that Sprint employee is what became the inspiration for my YouTube video entitled "Sprint Prostitute." As I stated before, I took Spanish for a number of years in school. As anyone can tell you about learning a foreign language, the first thing you typically learn is all the curse words! Now I admit, the call quality was a little shoddy and at best, it may be a little hard to determine whether the representative called me or someone else a whore. In any case after having two friends review the audio (one of whom is Mexican and the other lives abroad in Spain) it was determined that the representative was most likely referring to me as a whore in Spanish.

In my opinion it really doesn't matter. The fact that she was saying the word "whore" (whether in Spanish or not) while on the phone with a customer is unacceptable. What's even more unacceptable is that once she realized that I indeed spoke Spanish she immediately blind-transferred my call (sent it to another department) in an attempt to evade responsibility. I admit, initially I was very angry, but who wouldn't be? Shortly after I came to see the humor in the situation. So much so, that I located a website called GoAnimate.com and used their free trial to make a little cartoon about the incident. I then used their program to synchronize the call audio to the cartoon. It turned out so well that I decided to post that cartoon video to YouTube on February 22nd (2015). I was rather successful in my efforts of garnishing a few good laughs from people I knew at the time.

Now, I have worked in retention services at a major call center before and I know how customers can be. However, I also know that you don't curse at or in front of customers either. I personally would never call for someone to be fired over something so silly, but I do find it highly disappointing that Sprint to this day has never bothered to reach out to me with an apology. I also find it very disappointing that Sprint still hasn't provided me with my own phone records. In order to have them for the hearing I had to tell my lawyer to tell Justin Brown. I had to give Justin Brown permission to subpoena my own Sprint records.

Ironically it wasn't until the day after the hearing and after the "Sprint Prostitute" video started to go viral that Sprint reached out to me of their own accord. I think it was via some sort of automated Sprint Twitter customer satisfaction response system. Once again they asked about the problem, but this time I referred them to the video, my account notes and the Facebook Messenger thread of months and months of dialogue with various Sprint employees. Since that dialogue, I have yet to hear from Sprint again. As I sit here writing this now, no one from Sprint has provided me with my own phone records.

Believe it or not, over the last seventeen years this case is not something so easily forgotten. Every few years either in memory or activity, there is something that has resonated with me for one reason or another. I have a paper ream box in my basement with all my high school stuff in it. From photos to greeting cards, to journals and other keepsakes, it's all there. Every time this case comes up I eventually end up looking through that box again. Sometimes doing this causes me to get really nostalgic, and sometimes I find something I hadn't found before. It was during one of these moments that I stumbled across the "Urick notations" tucked inside my high school senior book. Needless to say I was freakin' ecstatic when I found them, because it was purely accidental that I came across them. I had forgotten all about them.

My husband and I moved (October 2015) a couple months after the private investigator came to our home in Oregon. As I stated before, we wanted to be closer to family, so we packed away our belongings and moved to Washington state. I believe it was at the tail end of 2015 (December) and I had already heard Urick's post-conviction testimony on SERIAL. I had just retained Gary Proctor and was about to start the task of writing my new affidavit. As soon as I discovered the notations tucked inside my senior book, I made it a point to tell my lawyer's associate

(Ali) about the find. My legal team then forwarded a copy of the document to both Vignarajah and Brown at the same time.

Many people have questions as to who wrote my second affidavit. Was it myself or was it my attorney? To best answer your question I would say that Ali gave me an affidavit template and then I took that document and completely spun it on its head. Writing my second affidavit was a very long and arduous process. It's something that meant a lot to me, so I took a lot of time getting it right. To be precise it actually took me twenty-four days. Much of that editing time was spent deleting, adding and rewriting wording. I would then send it to my lawyer for feedback and suggestions. I must have sent revisions to Ali and Gary about twelve times before it was completely done. It got to the point where my emails started to have subject lines like "You should know it's the affidavit by now." Initially I wanted to put all the information from my notes into the affidavit, but after thinking about it and discussing it with my lawyer, we felt that they would be too distracting from my overall goal. As a compromise between my heart and my head, I conceded to merely make mention of them in the affidavit. That way if the notes were ever needed to further explain things (in court), then they would not be anything unexpected to the court. Had I gone with my original instinct and infiltrated the contents of the notes into that document, it would have read a little something like this:

28. He told me that Adnan Syed had killed Hae Min Lee.

Urick told me that Mr. Brown did not have any open cases for Adnan and that they are just fishing for anything as a last resort before this May (when 10 years is up). Urick told me that within the first 10 years of a life sentence a person can reopen their case if they have new evidence. The defendant can only do this if it's within the first 10 years and if they have exhausted all their appeals and have no other recourse. He also told me there was no merit to any claims that CG was incompetent despite her health issues. I was fully assured that Brown would have no case in that matter.

Urick discussed the evidence of the case and everything he told me indicated that Syed was guilty. He told me that Jay testified to having helped bury Hae's body and that cell phone records indicated that the calls were coming from the area where they found her body. Urick said, "If I had any doubt that Adnan didn't kill Hae, it would be my moral obligation to see that he didn't serve any time" and "Oh, he killed that girl" and "There is a snowball's chance in hell that they could reopen the case with all the accusations that you're talking about, let alone get him off." Finally, he told me that at the time of the trial, Adnan had a bunch of witnesses ready to testify to him being at the mosque on that day, at that time; however, they all backed down once the cell phone records were proved. Kevin Urick convinced me not to bother participating in the case by telling what I knew about January 13th.

29. Urick and I discussed the affidavit I had previously pro-
vided to Chaudry. I wanted to know why I was being contacted if
they had the affidavit, and the ramifications of the document. I
never told Urick that I wrote my letter to Syed because of pressure
from the family. I never wrote anything to please the family and
get them off my back. What actually happened is that I wrote
the affidavit because I wanted to provide the truth about what I
remembered.

It was only after I considered typing all that did I realize
how combative, long and exhausting it all sounded. My lawyer
agreed. I mulled it over and decided not to "go there," mainly
because as I had reminded myself, my goal was to provide the
truth about what I had remembered about January 13th, 1999.
In fact, that very thought is what led me to add that very statement into the affidavit itself. After talking my thoughts over
with my attorney, he again agreed. "We need to stay focused," he
said. We both also came to the conclusion that it was absolutely
necessary to explain the context of my conversation with Kevin Urick. That way the court would understand Kevin Urick's
candor and comments were the sole reason that the defense was
unable to obtain my testimony (despite their very courageous
attempt to hire a private investigator). That's why I merely
alluded to my notations in my affidavit. I figured that my final
affidavit statement spoke to the context of my conversation with
Urick. I was also clear and to the point. I didn't want to call

Urick names or make speculations about his character. I didn't want to speculate on his intentions for testifying at the original post-conviction hearing or play the "he said, she said game." It was my belief that if the court needed more specific information, then the court could request the notations from my attorney, and at that time I would be more than happy to provide them.

On another note, I also didn't want to put all my eggs in one basket. I instinctively knew Urick would deny the context of our conversation. What I didn't know was whether or not he'd also try to publicly attack me somehow. I figured that perhaps if Urick became aware that I had specifics about our conversation, but not an idea of which specifics, then he would have more pause about retaliating. I also didn't want him to get a head start on verbally wiggling his way out of what he'd done either. I figured for the time being that keeping that info to myself was best because if the notations became public, I wanted him to be caught off-guard by them. My hope was that maybe then he'd slip up and incriminate himself. Little did I know, TheBlaze had unknowingly done that legwork for me. With the mere mention of our conversation, Urick immediately downplayed it and pegged himself into a five-minute conversation with me. In my opinion, this greatly shows to what length he does not remember our conversation correctly.

People have often said that my notes don't prove a thing. However, to me they prove a lot. As you can see from looking at them, some of the notations are direct quotes and some of the notations are paraphrases. Most of what is written in the notations is what could be construed as public knowledge. Jay was a witness, there were cell phone records, etc. However, there is one big piece of information in the notations that was not public knowledge in 1999, 2000 or 2010 for that matter—something that no one outside of myself, Phillip, Gary and Ali would (until now) deem suspicious. In Kevin Urick's Intercept interview dated January 7th, 2015, it can be noted that the article stated the following:

"Early on in the case, Urick said, the defense sent a disclosure to the state saying it had more than eighty witnesses who would testify about Adnan's whereabouts on the day he allegedly killed Hae and buried her body. But when the defense found out that the cellphone records showed that Adnan was nowhere near the mosque, it killed that alibi and those witnesses were never called to testify at the trial, according to Urick."

The thing that's interesting about this statement to me is that in the article it is says that Kevin Urick uses the description "eighty witnesses" to describe the individuals not used as alibis for Adnan Syed (in October of 1999.) Ironically, the first phone conversation that I had with my lawyer's legal associate Ali took place on December 20th, 2014—eighteen days before Urick's Intercept interview. In that conversation with Ali, I told her about finding the notes. I read to her everything from the page including the following notation:

"Bunch of witnesses ready to testify that he was at mosque [but they] backed down after cell records [disclosed]."

Now I know that I can't really prove that this happened. The closest that I've come is finding an email to my lawyer on January 12th where I talk about having told Ali eighteen days before the Intercept interview. So I can understand if you don't believe me, but what about Ali? It's one weird thing that I knew of the mere existence of these witnesses. Remember, these people never testified at trial and I never followed the trial anyway. It was another weird thing considering this now publicly disclosed document was not even available on the Internet at the time of my discussion with Ali. The most damning part (to me and my legal team) is the fact that I told Ali that I remembered Kevin Urick telling me there were "eighty people" who the defense never called as alibis.

Now I ask you this: how in the hell would I know that there were specifically "eighty people" who never testified in court? It's not likely that I would have been privy to any information discussed between the prosecution and the defense back at the time of Adnan's trial. Also, how in the hell would I know about it almost a whole month before Kevin Urick disclosed that information in his interview on January 7th? Finally, don't you find it a little odd that in that same article Urick claims that our phone conversation lasted only five minutes and that he never offered any trial information to me outside of stating that the prosecution indeed had a strong case? I beseech you (I'm kidding), but does that not sound like bullshit to you?! I'm just happy that Urick's narrative didn't succeed this time around. I've never met Kevin Urick and my hope is that I never do. Whatever his motivations and intentions were, it is my opinion that the truth was resilient and the truth prevailed.

CHAPTER SEVEN

LIFE AFTER/DURING SERIAL

This entire experience has been quite bizarre. Frankly it continues to get more surreal by the day. Sometimes it feels like a dream. Like something that is not really happening to me, but to someone else and I'm watching. One day you're a kid waiting for a ride in the library and the next you're on national television. I think one fact that helped me to retain some anonymity for such a long time is the fact that Asia McClain is now my maiden name. Per my request all parties involved kept the mention of my married name out of the media as long as they could. It literally was not until 2016, just weeks before the post-conviction hearing, did I tell anyone involved that my name is Asia Chapman. I'm sure they knew beforehand, but nobody ever spoke of it. In that regard everyone was very respectful of my privacy. Continuing to be referred to by my maiden name was a double-edged sword. Often times I felt like it has created a sense of dissociation from this case that often made things feel even more surreal. At times it felt like Asia McClain was a whole other person. As you can imagine, sometimes that made it harder to grasp the reality of why I felt certain emotions.

It's my belief that when you get married and take on your spouse's name that you do become someone different. You may not realize it at first, but you are starting a personal journey that will inevitably change more than your signature. I was married in 2009 and since then my husband and I have both grown to become better people. Every time I read my maiden name on the Internet, the person that I think about seems further and further away from the person that I am today. I don't consider infamy to be prize-worthy. Especially in today's age of Internet stalkers, bloggers and online comment threads. A few close friends who know the situation often ask what it's like and the best word I can use to describe it is bizarre.

It's bizarre to be internationally known for telling the truth. It's bizarre to have to scrub your personal contact information from the Internet every other week. It's bizarre not to know if some paparazzi person is going to jump out of your bushes and try to snap a current photo of you. It's bizarre to know that I'm a part of a Wikipedia entry or that my teenage letters to a classmate from over a decade ago are plastered all over the Internet. It's bizarre to know that millions of people that I don't know and have never met have such strong opinions about my character, my intelligence and my motives. That they are all either praising or judging me. I could go on for days about the bizarre aspects of this experience.

It's hard sometimes to wrap my head around the fact that I have to go above and beyond just to do the right thing. Really makes you wonder about the world that we live in nowadays. A totally objective, honest person can come forward with some truthful information, and be totally cut down by prosecutors and the naysayers of social media. It's truly sad when you think about it. I knew something was not right when the discussion of whether I needed character witnesses came up.

The nature of being cross-examined is something that I had to prepare myself for. I had to cultivate the intestinal fortitude to subject myself to and survive accusations and biased scrutiny. I had to mentally be prepared for possibly asinine accusations and offensive character smashing. It is as if I had to be willing to enter into the boxing ring unaware of my opponent's strength, tactics and strategies. That in itself was the most intimidating part. That is the fear that I had to overcome the most.

I will admit, there are a couple of other grievances that I had about the SERIAL podcast. The first is that the timeline of Sarah's evidentiary findings are somewhat jumbled up. For instance, in the podcast Sarah makes it seem as if she located Derrick and Jerrod prior to speaking with me. This is simply not true. In actuality, the first day I spoke with Sarah, she asked if I knew how to locate the two. In addition to sending her links that I had found for the Facebook profiles of both Jay Wilds and Jenn Pusateri, I sent Jerrod a message on Facebook and gave Sarah the location of Jerrod's Baltimore-based business. I believe it was sometime in April that Sarah located and interviewed Jerrod. That same day in January, I'd also given Sarah the house location for Derrick's mother. I gave her the names of all of Derrick's previous employers and a month later in February, she was able to reach him for his interview.

It wasn't until after the 2016 post-conviction hearing that I was able to speak with Derrick in person. The first thing I asked him was if he really didn't remember seeing Adnan in the library. Unfortunately, Derrick really doesn't remember seeing him now, but he trusts that if I said it happened, then it happened.

As far as Jerrod goes, he has yet to speak to me since our Facebook conversation in July of 2011. In any case, Derrick was both astonished and embarrassed to learn his interview with Sarah Koenig was featured in an internationally broadcasted podcast. He is not tech savvy in the slightest and tends to stay "off grid" (doesn't use Internet, email, etc.) a lot. As a result, he didn't even know what a podcast was. Apparently he had also made the same assumption about Sarah's recording desires as I had in 2014. Until I told him, he had never heard about SERIAL before. After I told him about it he was fascinated and said that he was going to check it out. He later reported that he was having technical issues and couldn't get the audio to play. Go figure.

The other bone that I have to pick with the SERIAL team is in regard to another editing decision. It really burns my biscuits that they completely edited Sarah's conversation with Jerrod. In the podcast interview they caught Jerrod making a funny joke in reference to my name. We all know the joke. It's the one where Jerrod says:

"I have no idea. Asia McClain? Is that a person or a book?"

Now I confirmed from Sarah that Jerrod did know who I was, but the editing team loved the joke so much that they decided to go with it. I can understand the humor in it, but I think it would have been a better choice to relay the fact that Jerrod did remember me. He was just not able to remember January 13th, 1999. When I first heard the joke, it really pissed me off. I think the thing that pisses me off the most about it was that I was Derrick's girlfriend for about three years, during and after high school. I saw Jerrod several times a week if not almost every day. To me, I initially thought Jerrod had lied to Sarah about not remembering me. The comment highly confused me because just two and a half years prior to interviewing with Sarah, I had found Jerrod through a mutual friend on Facebook. I sent him a message and we had an extensive conversation. In the conversation Jerrod confirmed that he knew exactly who I was.

I told him to say hello to Derrick for me. I told him about my family and where I was living. Jerrod responded by telling me about his business and that he was still single, but looking for that "special lady." Jerrod even said that he still saw Derrick about once a week and that he would tell him hello for me. So the fact that I thought Jerrod was now playing dumb, two and a half years later, made me feel very cross with him. It made me question whether Jerrod was avoiding telling the truth for some reason. It also made me question if he was lying about his memory of January 13th, 1999.

Back in 1999 when Adnan was arrested, both Derrick and Jerrod confirmed with me that they remembered seeing Adnan with me the library on January 13th, 1999. After Adnan's arrest I remember having a conversation in which I said to them, "Hey, do you guys remember that guy that I was talking to in the public library the day you picked me up at school?" They both responded, "Yeah." I then said, "Well, he just got arrested for killing his ex-girlfriend." They both responded by saying, "Damn! For real?!"

I never told them that Adnan was suspected of killing Hae that same day, because at the time I didn't wholeheartedly believe that to be the case. So fast-forward to me listening to the SERIAL podcast in 2014 and hearing them both say the opposite. My anger and suspicion got to the point where I typed up a long message to Sarah explaining that Jerrod was a liar and that he knew exactly who I was. I got on my cell phone and took a screenshot of the Facebook conversation that I had with Jerrod. I attached it to the email and right before I was about to send it I stopped. I stopped because I realized how petty my email sounded, so instead I picked up the phone and gave Sarah a call. We talked about a few things—nothing important—and then I casually mentioned the part about Jerrod in the podcast. Right as I was attempting to tell her that I had contacted Jerrod in 2011, she stopped me. With laughter in her voice she said something to the effect of, "Yeah, we kind of edited it that way. We thought it was kind of funny so we kept it. Later on in the conversation, he did come around and eventually admitted that he did know who you were." I just thank God that I expressed my frustration with Sarah before approaching Jerrod with my accusations! Now don't get me wrong; like I said, I can totally see the humor in that part of the podcast. However as "Asia McClain" it became somewhat insulting. I think if nothing else, they should have come out with the truth later (as to not disturb the moment of the humor) I only say this because it caused me to become the brunt of endless Internet ridicule.

"Was she that forgettable in high school?" (spinning the "Adnan crush" and case insertion theories)

"Asia McClain, that's not really a person, that's a TV show!"

"No wonder Adnan couldn't even remember talking to her in the library that day! Jerrod is Asia's ex-boyfriend's best friend and he couldn't even remember her!"

I have pretty thick skin, but I still hate comments like those. They are belittling and during the beginning, there was a time when they hurt my feelings.

Let's take a moment to put a few things into perspective here. I wasn't aware that Sarah would be using the recording for her podcast. I wasn't aware that my answers would be taken so literally. As a result, I allowed myself to speculate, when I really should not have.

Asia McClain: "...I remember that day, because that was the day that it snowed."

Sarah Koenig: "Were there snow days after that, do you remember?"

Asia McClain: "I want to say there was, because *I think* that was '*like*' the first snow of the year. I wouldn't have even remembered if it hadn't have been for the 'snow.' And the whole—I just remember being so pissed about Derek being late and then getting 'snowed in' at his house. And it was the first snow of that year."

My comments to Sarah about January 13th's weather were intended as a candid guess about the type of weather that caused our two-day school closing (in 1999). In addition, it was the best guess of a person fifteen years after the fact. It wasn't meant to be taken as testimony and I was never certain about it enough to offer it as testimony. Thus why in my 2015 affidavit I clarified my language, in an attempt to be as accurate as possible about what it was that I actually remembered. In terms of my interview with Sarah, I think the more important issue that I am absolutely certain of is that the bad weather resulted in two days of school closings. The other funny thing about that statement is that there is a part where there lies a lost thought.

"...And the whole— ..."

Had I actually finished my thought in that sentence, that lost thought would have sounded more like this:

"...And the whole fact that I remember thinking that's why they [the police] found Hae in a shallow grave! The ground was too frozen to dig the grave!"

I don't know if that addition would have made any difference in people's opinion. My "guestimation" about whether it was snow or ice is debatable and to some, flat out wrong. It apparently wasn't the first snow of the year, so I was wrong there. Perhaps those two days that school was closed were the first "snow days" of 1999? I'm not 100 percent sure, but then again, this is me trying to recall the weather conditions over fifteen years after the fact. What I can tell you is that in 1999, I specifically remember seeing and speaking to Adnan Syed in that library. After his arrest, I do remember making a correlation between the weather, Hae's shallow grave, that day being the last time Hae or Adnan had crossed my mind (before her disappearance) and having two snow days off from school. I remember that along with feeling neglected, then angry, then smitten with Derrick (yes, all in the course of one day. Hello, I was a teenage girl!), and that all of these things are a result of what I experienced on January 13th, 1999.

While we're discussing the weather, let me clarify another thing. I never said I spent the night at my then-boyfriend's house on the night of January 13th. I believe that was Rabia Chaudry who said that in the podcast. I did use the words "snowed in" but where I'm from, that doesn't indicate a specific amount of time. I never intended for anyone to think I was implying that I had spent the night at Derrick's house. By no means did the weather cause me to get stuck at Derrick's house overnight. I was merely there past my typically allowed curfew, and therefore I had to call my mom for an extension. The weather merely served as the reasoning behind that. As I stated in court, my mom "bought it," so I was able to squeeze in a little more time with my boyfriend. This notion that as a teenager, I somehow was allowed to sleep over my boyfriend's house is so ridiculous! I don't know what kind of mothers you guys have and what kind of mother you think I have, but that would never be allowed. My mom would not be having that—at all. My mom didn't know Derrick's mother or how well supervised we were. She would have never been comfortable with an overnight scenario! Derrick lived a good ten-minute drive (or thirty to forty-five-minute walk) from my house. I'd venture to say that worst-case scenario, my mother would have come to pick me up herself. Really worst-case scenario, she would have told me to get my ass outside and start walking! The truth is that I simply used the weather as an excuse to barter more time at Derrick's house. I don't recall what the time was when I finally got home, but I know it was very late because I remember being both extremely sleepy and happy that school was closed when I awoke that morning.

CHAPTER EIGHT

THE 2016 POST-CONVICTION HEARING

November 6th, 2015, is the day I found out about the motion to re-open Adnan Syed's post-conviction proceedings. Ever since my earlier January 2015 affidavit I was aware of the possibility of such an outcome. However, when I received the email from Gary Proctor telling me that it was official, the reality came with a wave of mixed emotions. In the email, Gary informed me that I would soon need to visit the east coast. Later that day, as I read a copy of the official motion, I began to understand that the post-conviction relief request had more parts to it than just requesting my testimony. I came to understand that the defense was beginning to call into question the reliability of the 1999 cell phone records used to convict Syed in 2000. I'd be lying to say that information didn't make me feel somewhat less stressed because at least the post-conviction wasn't all about me.

Unfortunately, with the stress level that I was functioning at, the decrease was pitifully minute. I was elated at the prospects of getting the truth to the court, however the scrutiny of all the media attention was definitely not something that I looked forward to. I can remember asking both my husband and my lawyer how bad they thought it was going to be. My lawyer responding by saying something like, "All's well that ends with someone not peering in through your bushes...If it happens, it happens. You can't really stop that kind of thing nowadays."

I remember constantly telling my husband to make sure that our blinds in the living room were closed because of concern that a weird person could be skulking around our home trying to catch a photo or two. On a funny note I can recall telling a friend about that concern and having him joke about me going to the grocery store in high heels, wearing a big hat and huge sunglasses, as to "not be getting caught out there like Britney Spears." In any case, the invasive nature of the media was a big concern to my husband and me.

I can recall fearing the prospect of the media getting wind of our arrival date/time and invading our privacy both at the airport and/or where we would be staying once in Baltimore. We didn't know what to expect. To make matters worse, the Paris terrorist attacks happened and I started getting weird cryptic Facebook messages from strangers about helping out a Muslim.

All the while I was accompanied by the fear of Jay Wilds (his involvement scares me) being in Baltimore and possibly in attendance at the hearing. As the arrival date began to get closer and closer, I affectionately started referring to the post-conviction hearing as "The Freak Show." People on the Internet were referring to my upcoming testimony as the second coming of Christ for SERIAL disciples. The idea of being paraded around as some sort of "white whale" was not appealing to me in the slightest. Everybody said to ignore it all. "Just put on your blinders," one friend said. "How do you do that when it's hitting you from all angles?" I replied.

That's not to say that my only concerns were for my own wellbeing either. In the days that followed I worried a lot about the impact all of this was having on the Lee family and their friends. I wondered if they hated me for coming forward. For giving the man that they perceive as being Hae's murderer a slight window of hope. Once again I started to feel the tug of two family's convictions pulling at me and weighing on my heart. Not only did the families weigh on me. Adnan and Hae weighed on me as well. What if Adnan was the killer and somehow I was a ploy? What if Adnan was innocent and this was indeed setting things right? Then again what if I wasn't? Was Hae rolling in her grave or was she cheering me on? I tried to block those thoughts from my head, but try as I may I could not. In addition, my Ulcerative Colitis was in full swing, probably due to all of my stress, and I had recently found out that I was pregnant.

Earlier that year I had lost two babies and the prospect of all the ongoing stress associated with traveling and the hearing itself was not welcomed at all. After miscarrying two babies, my spirit had been severely shattered and I had become paranoid and convinced that everything I did was going to cause a third miscarriage. Hell, at the time I was so frightful that I couldn't even discuss my fears with my husband because I was too afraid that just talking about it was bad luck. I stopped going to the gym, I stopped going most places; I just stayed home and worried. As you can imagine the thought of a lingering undetermined travel date only added to my worry. In the weeks that followed my lawyer and I would discuss my pregnancy in terms of when I would be available to testify and when I would not. We would talk about Justin Brown and Thiru Vignarajah. We would talk about current events and weather systems that could possibly affect the scheduling of the hearing. Gary would assure me that it would all work out. "They hate closing court. Even if schools are closed and federal court is closed a lot of time the Baltimore city circuit court is still open," he said.

Initially we thought that perhaps the hearing would happen in March of the next year, but we were unsure. All we knew for sure was that it couldn't be between mid-April and the second week of July (because of my pregnancy). As time passed I became more aware that the hearing was going down sooner rather than later. When it came to finding out the actual hearing date, I think I found out via the Internet before I found out from my attorney. It was December 15th, 2015, and being the person that I am, I had previously set up a Google alert for any news containing my name. That day I received an email with a link to a news article in which the scheduled hearing date had been disclosed. After sending Gary a quick text, he was able to confirm and soon after, I started to receive emails about travel arrangements. Before I knew it my flight was booked, and I was making arrangements for dog sitting. Unfortunately, the hearing dates soon proved to be inconsistent. Eleven days later I received another text from Gary stating that the hearing dates had been moved up a few days from their original schedule. Normally this would not have been a big deal, but the Alaska Airlines plane tickets were non-refundable. Luckily I was able to investigate their ticket change policy and they did permit for a one-time-only ticket change on non-refundable tickets. The only thing left to do at that point was to prepare for my first (and probably most important) court testimony ever.

Once all the travel arrangements were set in stone, I became more comfortable with the premise of testifying and being cross-examined. The only court experience that I had was when I received a ticket for expired license plate tags. I had to go before a judge to show my updated license plate information. That court appearance resulted in me getting out of my legal pickle so I chalk that up to being a success. This experience, however, was going to be something totally different. The only thing I had to compare what this experience could be like was television. No matter what people say, television is where reality goes to die nowadays. That being the case, I had no clue what to expect. To what degree would the defense try and sell me down the road on this whole alibi thing? How mean would Vignarajah actually be to me? I had already had one bad experience with a prosecutor, so the idea of speaking with another was intimidating. Even so, I knew in my heart that I couldn't hold my reservations about the whole Urick incident against Vignarajah and I didn't. Ironically though, Vignarajah apparently never had a desire to speak with me because my personal invitation to him was ignored. Since this information was unforeseen in those moments, Gary and I deemed it a better focus of my time to go over the previous documents that I had presented to the court so that my recollection of writing them and their content would be fresh in my mind. Considering that it had been almost sixteen years since my first affidavit was written, I saw the value in this task.

While going over these documents I soon realized that my age was beginning to show in the sense that I would misspeak years when referring to certain events. Nothing important, but still not something that I wanted to screw up in court. We all know what it's like at the first of the year when it's the New Year and you're still writing last year's date on your checks. Those kinds of mistakes, nothing major. Nevertheless, I continued to be very hard on myself. Gary told me over and over again to relax, that court was going to be boring and nothing like the movies. He assured me that Vignarajah was not going to yell and scream at me while I was on the stand. I admit, looking back I was an absolute train wreck. The rational part of my brain trusted Gary's courtroom knowledge and experience, but there was a definite irrational side to my brain that was obviously a little out of control.

Being that I was raised in Baltimore I still have a lot of personal connections there. Many of my friends are well-paid professionals and some are even stewards of the court. In my various conversations with my friends in Baltimore, Thiru Vignarajah had been described to me in a not-so-flattering light. I'm not the type to hold grudges against people, especially those that I don't have personal relationships with, but I was worried. I had been told that he was wicked smart and that he was often willing to win his cases at any cost. I had been told that he appeared to lack a moral compass when it came to his courtroom tactics. I had been told about the www.projectveritas.com scandal and warned that he was the type to smile in your face while stabbing you in the back. Needless to say, I became scared of him, or better yet, the idea of somebody who was how he had been described to me.

The Defense

I'll never forget the first time I met Justin Brown. To say the least, he's very different than what I expected back in 2010. Before speaking to him in 2016, I had always imagined him to be this smooth-tongued, conniving defense attorney. Along with the help of Kevin Urick, I had made the wrongful assumption that someone of his professional standing must have possessed a low, or no, standard of morality. After all, he does represent some of society's worst criminals for a living. In short, I was pleasantly surprised to discover that he was down to earth, very soft-spoken (when not in court) and not very intimidating at all (in a good way). I found him to be extremely patient and respectful of my family and my time. I admit, a lot of his candor toward my husband and myself may have been in light of my recent commitment to writing a new affidavit and my participation in general. Notwithstanding those facts, I got the feeling that he had a healthy sense of humor and was generally a nice person. I think the first time we met he just mainly wanted to put eyes on me. He had spent such a long time seeking out the testimony of the elusive Asia McClain and to put it plainly, I think he just needed to see me with his own eyes. I can't say that I blame him.

The experience was very bizarre for me as well. Immediately, the first thing I did was apologize to him about not reaching back out to him in 2010. By that time, Justin had already read my new (2015) affidavit and was already aware of the original post-conviction hearing back-story (Urick). He graciously accepted my apology and we agreed to move forward. He explained the date of my testimony and the fact that my husband would be listed on the witness list. He explained that he wanted me to be aware of this fact because most likely all the witnesses involved would be under a sequestration. As I'm sure you all know, a sequestration basically means that one witness cannot be present in the courtroom while another is testifying. It also means that witnesses are not supposed to read or watch anything pertaining to the statements of other witnesses and that they also cannot discuss the case in general for fear of influencing changes in one another's testimony.

In all honesty I'd have to say this was the hardest part of the entire post-conviction hearing process. My husband is my best friend and a major support system in my life. The fact that I had to endure a day and a half of testifying and cross-examination all by myself royally sucked. To make matters worse, I wasn't even allowed to discuss details of the hearing with him (or anyone else for that matter) until after the hearing was concluded. My husband and I agreed to follow the rules of the sequestration, should it be put into place by Vignarajah. Justin then informed me that he was able to obtain my Sprint phone records and I was elated. Up to that point, I had tried unsuccessfully for about a year to obtain my own phone records, only to come up empty-handed. Justin was able to get a subpoena and obtain the records within a span of two or three days.

After he handed me the records I proceeded to flip through the pages until I came to page three of thirty-six. On that page in plain sight was my call to Kevin Urick dated April 11th, 2010, and right there in plain sight was a call duration time of thirty-four minutes. I have to admit, in that moment I felt vindicated. For more than a year I had felt certain that the representation of my phone call with Kevin Urick had been greatly distorted from the truth. I had also been aware that the length of the actual phone call had been greatly undercut and extremely underestimated. For the first time in over a year I finally had proof! I can remember thinking that if only for my own peace of mind, I was so happy to finally have proof!

As we continued our conversation everything else felt null in terms of my excitement. Justin asked me a variety of questions concerning my involvement in the case. He asked me if I was indeed the Asia McClain that saw Adnan Syed in the library on January 13th, 1999. I thought it would be funny to mess with him, so I replied, "No." We all laughed but you could tell that, as he took a huge breath of relief, the joke had momentarily panicked him. The split-second expression on his face was indeed quite priceless. I explained my story of January 13th to Justin and how it corresponded with my affidavit from early 2000. He asked me about my letters to Adnan dated March 1st and 2nd of 1999 and I explained them to him the same way I explained them earlier in this book. He asked me if I had ever been asked or felt pressured by Adnan or the Syed family to write anything; I responded by telling him that I had not. Mr. Brown then asked my husband and me if we were aware that an individual had attempted to serve me a subpoena back in 2010 and we were shocked. We explained that I had become a stay-at-home wife the year before in June and that at no point had anyone ever (to our knowledge) come to our home trying to serve me. We also explained that a few months later we moved out of state and perhaps that was the reason we were unreachable for service. After that, I asked Mr. Brown if Kevin Urick was going to testify at the hearing and he informed me that Kevin Urick was listed as a witness, but that he did not know if the State would call him to testify. Nonetheless, he assured me not to worry about it, because he felt as though he was well-prepared for a multitude of possible scenarios.

The Prosecution

As far as Thiru Vignarajah goes, I don't know what to make of him personally. Like I said earlier, my lawyer Gary Proctor ran into Vignarajah in downtown Baltimore (while working) and extended a personal invitation for Thiru to speak with me before the post-conviction hearing. Gary let Vignarajah know that I was not taking sides with either the prosecution or defense teams and that I would be more than willing to participate any questioning. As far as my lawyer has told me, Vignarajah (unlike

Justin Brown) never called to request my time. With that being said if I were to go by how Vignarajah treated me before the trial, I'd say my opinion is he is a very nice and polite man. If I were to go by how he treated me during my cross-examination, I'd say my opinion is he is annoying, manipulative and backhanded. If I were to go by the ways in which he has talked about me since the hearing, I'd say my opinion is that he is an asshole. Again, I get it. He has a job to do and he does it well. I just wonder how he can be so inconsiderate and cold-hearted about it. It's almost like he has a built-in treachery switch. I probably should have gotten a clue the Saturday before the post-conviction hearing when my friend Stacie called me to tell me about some of Vignarajah's antics.

The night I arrived in Baltimore for the hearing, Stacie called me very upset because a plain-clothes police officer showed up at her house after 10 PM that night. According to Stacie, she was home alone when the man banged on her front door both scaring her and waking up her three young children. Upon cracking the door open, the strange man informed her that his name was Mark Veney and he was a homicide detective from the Baltimore City Police Department. Stacie said that instantly her heart dropped as she immediately thought someone had been murdered (but who!?). The officer then informed her that he was sent by the Deputy Attorney General Thiru Vignarajah, and that he had questions surrounding the death of a young lady named Hae Min Lee. After stumbling to pronounce Hae and Adnan's names, he continued to say that he was aware that Stacie had attended Woodlawn during the time of Hae's murder and that the nature of his visit surrounded information that Stacie might have from 1999. The detective then stated the fact that Syed's lawyer had noted her name on his witness list. At that point Stacie knew what the detective was talking about, and she became rightfully irritated and angry with both the detective and Vignarajah.

Previous to all of this I had spoken to Stacie about the hearing and whether she would agree to be on the witness stand (she agreed). Much like Rabia Chaudry, Stacie was never called upon in court but the state still had to have her on the witness list in case they needed her testimony. Nonetheless, Stacie told me the detective continued to seek answers from her even though he didn't seem to have a strong grasp on his assignment directives. As her children cried in the background, Stacie said she expressed to the detective that she was insulted by the time of night that he had chosen to visit her. She said he apologized and then admitted that he was merely "doing the foot work" and that he was not very knowledgeable about the purpose of the line of questioning. Stacie told me she refused him entry into her home, so he then slid his hand through the opening in her screen door. He handed her a cell phone, which placed her on the line with Vignarajah.

According to Stacie, Vignarajah then had the audacity to attempt to continue following through with his questioning, as if what he had just facilitated wasn't rude, intimidating or—at best—just plain tacky. God forbid Vignarajah get his own ass out of bed to interview witnesses after ten o'clock at night, but I digress. So anyway, naturally by this time, Stacie said that her young children were very upset and that she was both freaked out and highly irritated. As such, she immediately told Vignarajah that if he wanted to speak to her then he could do so at a respectable time of day and not at almost 11 PM at night (Go, Stacie! Right?!) According to Stacie, she then got some push back from Vignarajah; he wanted to know if she and I talked about the upcoming hearing. He wanted to know if she or anyone else had any specific nicknames (that he wouldn't mention) back in high school. Stacie admits that she did answer one or two of his questions but ultimately stuck to her guns about speaking to her at a decent time. They then made arrangements to speak the next day.

Stacie claims the next day Vignarajah came back with the homicide detective in tow. Right off the bat, Stacie said she scolded Vignarajah for contacting her after ten o'clock at night. He rebutted that it was before 9:30 and she corrected him by proclaiming that it was indeed definitely after ten o'clock at night when they spoke on the phone. She also told Vignarajah that the previous night's visit really made her uncomfortable so as a precaution, she wanted her children's grandmother to sit in on the conversation. Vignarajah apologized, agreed to Stacie's guest and proceeded to record her questioning. According to Stacie, Vignarajah asked if she remembered me telling her about my letters to Adnan in 1999. Stacie admitted that she doesn't have the best memory and indeed didn't remember much about the time after Adnan's arrest. "Asia has the best memory out of all my friends," she said. In addition, she told him that she remembered being saddened and shocked by the turn of events. Stacie then admitted to purposely trying not to remember details of that time, specifically because she was a friend to both Hae and Adnan and those thoughts are all together very troubling to her. Stacie said it was at this time that Vignarajah doubled down on the question and again Stacie told him the memories she did recall but reiterated that she didn't remember much. Then Vignarajah asked Stacie if she and I saw each other a lot during class back in high school. Stacie said she replied, "No." She also told him that she was in Woodlawn's magnet program and I was not, therefore we did not have classes together. She told him that we've been best friends since junior high and that in high school the bulk of our interaction was afterschool during sports and social activities. Stacie told me that she felt as if Vignarajah had hinted at wanting to know if she knew where I was staying while I was in town for the hearing (even though he already knew that I could be reached for questioning through my attorney). She then said that Vignarajah apologized to her for the last-minute questioning but stated that Adnan's defense team dragged their feet on providing him with her information and that it was difficult to locate her. Ultimately, she was "last on the list."

Finally, Stacie said that he asked if she has had any contact with Adnan's legal team. All in all, Stacie estimated the visit lasted about twenty minutes and Vignarajah was very intimidating. In her opinion, it seemed as if Vignarajah was trying to make me the enemy because of the possibility that the State got Adnan's conviction wrong back in 2000. She also admitted to me that the interview was not pleasant and not something she ever wants to do again.

In actuality the first time that I met Vignarajah was the first day of my testimony. My husband and I were waiting outside the courtroom with my attorney when Vignarajah and his entourage arrived. As I stared at the three attorneys approaching, Gary informed me that one of them (pointing to Vignarajah) was the prosecutor. As Vignarajah got closer I stood up, walked towards him, eagerly shook his hand and introduced myself. As expected he was extremely nice to me. He smiled and said how much of a pleasure it was to meet me. Little did I know at the time, he was not always going to be so nice. I had forgotten what my friend had told me about him smiling in your face while stabbing you in the back. Unbeknownst to me, within next forty-eight hours, that same man would refer to me as a liar and co-conspirator (to my face). In any regard, like I said, I had no idea at that time what he had in store for me and I had forgotten the warning I had been given. I simply smiled back and he walked away. The thing that I remember being most comical about that interaction was not Thiru himself, but the female African-American associate that accompanied him into court. As Vignarajah walked away she said something to the effect of, "Oh my God, I love your lipstick. Where did you get it?" I responded by telling her that I had received it from my friend back home but that it was from Stila Cosmetics and that it could be purchased at Sephora. She smiled and told me that she had just been there and had recently purchased some Stila products but was not familiar with the red color that I was wearing. I tried to tell her the name of the color (Beso) but it was at that instant that Vignarajah reappeared from beyond the courtroom doors. He sternly beckoned for her attention and presence. After the three attorneys were all safely inside the courtroom, Gary, my husband and myself all had a good chuckle about the interaction had just transpired.

"I hope you didn't get her in trouble," my husband snickered.

"Oops!" I giggled.

Before I knew it the first day of the post-conviction hearing was upon me. As you can imagine, I didn't sleep well the night before and yet somehow I woke up pumped and ready to go. As

I got prepared to leave I strangely started to think about television. I started to feel like I was in Hollywood cinema when one of the characters is awaiting the electric chair. I was confident that I was doing the right thing and told myself that the truth would prevail. However, the uncertainty of what would happen after I sat in the witness chair felt a lot like *The Green Mile*. After we arrived downtown and found parking, we met my attorney at a local Starbucks. Gary was dressed to the nines as usual: a fresh crisp suit with a coordinating Kangol hat to boot. My husband was dressed in his finest Jos. A. Bank solid black suit and black tie; myself in a two-piece zigzag-patterned Calvin Klein dress suit, red lips and non-matching multicolored umbrella that I had snagged from my grandmother the day before.

After purchasing a few breakfast treats we left and proceeded to walk to the courthouse. I remember that I had to be extra careful where I stepped. It was raining and the downtown sidewalks in Baltimore are especially treacherous in certain spots. *That's all I need, to stumble and bust my ass on camera,* I thought. To our relief when we approached the courthouse there were no cameramen in sight that first day. We stood in line, had our belongings searched and jumped on the elevator to go upstairs. Once we got up there, I began to feel nervous. There were plenty of people walking around and I couldn't tell who, if any, knew who I was.

As I got closer to the courtroom I noticed how beautiful the courthouse interior architecture actually was. There was white marble everywhere and wooden trim that had to have been very old and yet very well-preserved. As we walked down the hall towards the courtroom, I noticed signs everywhere. "No cell phones" said one. "No photography or audio recording devices" and so on. This of course pleased me because I didn't have to worry about people snapping photos of me, or so I thought. In any case, at one point I can remember seeing Rabia Chaudry talking to two other people. I immediately knew it was her because she looked just like I'd remembered her. It's weird and I don't know why I felt drawn to go speak to her, but I did not. I didn't know what the rules were for this kind of thing and I didn't think it would be appropriate. Fortunately for me, that was a good call because given the soon-to-be-placed sequestration, that would have not been a good thing for us to do. So instead, we caught eyes and smiled and went our separate ways.

Soon after, my husband and I plopped our butts on the wooden bench directly outside the right-hand-side courtroom door (where my poor husband would spend the next two days) and began the drudging task of waiting to be called. As we sat there many people passed us by. Many of which looked at us, hardly any of which spoke to us. Entirely all of which I didn't know and then I saw Sarah Koenig approach. When I saw Sarah she was in mid-conversation with another person so I didn't immediately get up from my seat. As I sat and watched I couldn't help but think that she looked exactly how I'd imagined her to look. That is, like every Internet photo I've ever seen of her. I believe she was dressed in a t-shirt and dark pants. Her hair, although beautifully wavy, wasn't especially done up and her face, although equally attractive, had little to no makeup at all. In that moment I found myself envying her because she looked so comfortable, where as I was pregnant, in a monkey suit and heels. As the person she had been talking to began to walk away, I stood up and yelled her name. She turned her gaze towards me, smiled and began to walk in my direction. I could tell that she had no idea who the hell I was. As a consequence, I was smiling and laughed as I shook her hand.

"Hi, it's Asia," I said.

"Oh!" she said. "Nice to officially meet you!"

"Finally!" I said. I then introduced my husband and Gary into the conversation. We chit-chatted about the fortuitous circumstances that had brought us both to court that day and with that she headed back into the courtroom. As my husband and I went back to sitting, he admitted that he had no idea who she was until I introduced him. I laughed and questioned how on earth it was that he didn't have a clue after all this time.

In any case, a significant amount of time went by in which my husband and I made friends with the sheriffs posted in front of the courtroom. Because there was no phone usage allowed we were "forced to actually talk to one another" as one of the sheriffs joked. Not being allowed into the courtroom was pretty agonizing and proved to be a complete waste of half a day. Before too long everyone began to reemerge from the courtroom. Unbeknownst to us, the judge had just called for a lunch recess and everyone was free to leave for a bit. Gary poked his head out of the courtroom and suggested that we meet him at the local café where we had met him a couple of days before. We agreed and continued on with the task of leaving the courthouse. Feeling famous is not something that feels great to me. That day was no exception.

As we walked the streets of downtown Baltimore I can remember being grateful for the rain. Ever since we arrived I was paranoid about public exposure and therefore I confided in the little shelter that my umbrella provided. Everywhere we went I feared that people would recognize me, stare or approach me. I know it was probably just my wild imagination, but that day it felt as if everyone was staring at me. Lunchtime was no exception. We made our way into the local café and purchased sandwiches and soup. Soon after, Gary appeared and sat along with us. Due to the sequestration Gary was unable to tell me about any of the earlier day's testimonies, so instead we focused on more important matters like how I was feeling and what I thought about the other events of the day so far. Gary assured me that I would do fine in court and before you knew it we were once again walking in the rain back to the courthouse.

Walking into the courtroom alone was one of the most alienating feelings that I have ever felt in my life. As I walked in and began to look for Gary, I could sense everyone's eyes on me. Scratch that. I could *see* that everyone was looking at me. I've been the center of attention before, but never in my life has it ever felt as intense as it was that day. As I made my way to the front of the courtroom I could tell that everybody was sizing me up. Everything from my red lipstick to the way I walked down the aisle was up for evaluation. As I looked around I could see that the courtroom had been basically split into thirds.

The far right third was comprised of Adnan's family and supporters. The middle third was full of Hae's and the far right third of the crowd consisted of the media and various spectators. I found my way to Gary and waited for the court session to begin. As everyone continued to be seated the back door to the far left of the courtroom opened and out of it appeared a female guard. Right behind her walked a shackled Adnan Syed. I tried not to look at him but the temptation was way too strong. I had not seen Adnan since he was a seventeen-year-old boy and now he was a thirty-five-year-old man. It was hard to tell if his time in prison had been kind to his face. The majority of the lower portion of his face was covered in a big dark beard. On the top was a blue and white crocheted kufi (hat). He definitely didn't look like he did in high school. He was much bigger and a little scary. Not in the "murderer way" kind of scary, but the "I've been in prison for sixteen years" kind of scary. Also, his face was quite blank and emotionless. I imagine that given the circumstances his expression should have been expected. In that moment, I can remember wondering if he had been instructed not to smile, or if he had been instructed not to look at me, because Lord knows he didn't even dare. Not to say that I minded either, it actually was a comfort. Definitely a strange feeling but way less strange than the possibility of locking eyes with him.

Even though I never made eye contact with him, I did make out the presence of his big "dairy cow eyes," only to me they weren't so "mooie." Sadder and filled with solace is a better description for his eyes that day. They made me wonder what was going on in his mind. What was he thinking? One can only imagine. As I continued to inspect his person, I couldn't help but notice that he was shackled and chained in four point restraints. Around his waist went a thick stainless steel chain and there looked to be a large padlock on the side. The way they had him shackled, his arms were not capable of extending and it looked as if they were almost crossed. The forced posture looked very uncomfortable and I can remember saying to Gary, "Geez, is that really necessary?"

In any case, he continued to approach with two guards, one female and the other a man. As they got closer to the defense team seating area, Gary tapped me on the shoulder and advised me to take a step back. Apparently there are a lot of unspoken rules when in court. One of which is don't let the defendant walk, stand or look anywhere near a witness, especially a potential alibi witness. From what I understand that was already an issue at trial. As Adnan positioned himself next to Justin Brown and Chris Nieto, the Honorable Judge Martin P. Welch appeared from his quarters and called the court into session. As I found myself mentally clinging to Gary for dear life I was then told by the judge that I could approach the witness stand. I did so, then took a seat and before I knew it my attraction in the freak show was set to begin.

There's no other way to say this. For me personally, testifying in this case was a royal bitch. I loathed almost every part of it. To start, the courtroom temperature was very inconsistent. One day it was warm enough to be considered a large sweat lodge, the next day I found myself testifying wearing Judge Welch's overcoat. In addition, the witness seating area is completely awkward and uncomfortable. The place where you sit down to testify consists of a little desk and chair at the front of the courtroom. To my left was Judge Welch and to my right were Adnan, Justin Brown and Chris Nieto. To the left of those three sat Vignarajah and his crew. So basically if you speak facing forward during your testimony, you're not directly facing anyone. In order to address the attorneys, you have to posture yourself slightly turned to the (right) side. I assume that perhaps in the case of a jury trial, you'd be looking straight ahead. In my case,

all I had were a couple of empty rows of seats and a large projector screen.

The other thing about the seating that sucks is the speaking podium is secured to the floor. Not that I would anticipate
moving the podium, but you'd think the chair would be slightly
more accommodating. Nope! There's no scooting yourself closer
to the podium because the chair is bolted in place to the floor.
Whoever designed that aspect of the courtroom esthetics needs
to be fired. The third thing that royally takes the cake is that
the podium microphone stem is so short that it's practically
non-existent. I testified for over six damn hours and the entire
damn time I was forced to sit on the edge of that uncomfortable
chair just to be effectively heard by that stupid microphone. As
you can see, just thinking about it now makes me mad. Imagine
sitting on the edge of a chair with no back support for over six
hours. That would be killer for anyone. Try doing it when you're
a couple months pregnant and have a little one stomping on your
bladder and other internal organs the whole time. Yeah, not fun.

My Testimony

Before I get into my testimony, let me preface it by saying that
this is my best recollection of the events. Not all of the quotes
will be verbatim. I know they should be but that's next to impossible without the actual court transcripts (which I don't have).
My memory is fairly good, but not that good! Needless to say, I'm
going to try and touch on everything that was said, but again,

that's pretty impossible given the amount of content to cover. I'm going to do my best to give as much detail as I can recall. Due to the way in which I was questioned, I can't guarantee that all of my versions will be in the same exact order it happened in court. Also, some things may not be addressed at all because they have already been addressed in other parts of this book. If you feel like my depiction of my testimony is not fulfilling enough for you, you are more that welcome to go purchase the court transcripts.

First up was the Syed defense team. Justin Brown stood up and asked me my name, to which I replied "Asia Chapman." He then asked if I had formerly been known as Asia McClain and if he could refer to me as Asia McClain for the duration of the hearing. Any time I hear "formerly known as" I automatically want to say Prince, but I digress. Although I wanted to say no, I obliged anyway to avoid making things more difficult. I've been married for almost seven years and I by no stretch of the imagination am anything close to the girl I was when I got married. Being a wife and mother has forced me to grow in ways that I could have only imagined and for that I love the name Asia Chapman. So when people refer to me as Asia McClain, I get it; however, there is a part of me that rejects that notion.

At any rate, Brown then began to ask me about my activities on January 13th, 1999. I explained to him my typical day and why January 13th was different. Then Brown placed an image of my 1999 cooperative education hall pass on the projector screen and asked me to read the time off the pass. "10:40 AM," I said. He asked me to oblige him by reading the dates on the pass. "November 10th, 1998 through May 21st, 1999," I responded.

As we moved on, I explained to him the circumstance that led me to engage in a fifteen- to twenty-minute conversation with Syed and what I took away from that chance encounter. I was informed later that the mere mention of this interaction made Adnan cry. Brown then asked about my perception of the Woodlawn campus and whether I considered the Public Library to be on the school grounds. "Oh, yeah!" I replied. To everyone that attended Woodlawn, if you were at the library, you were still at school. Hell, if you were at the diner or 7-11 across the street, for all intents and purposes you were still at school! Well, I guess I can't say *everyone* because Vignarajah graduated from Woodlawn the year prior to our freshman year in 1995. According to public opinion, he obviously doesn't consider the library as part of the high school campus, but I digress again.

Anyhow, I described as best I could the revelation about speaking to Syed on the very same day that Hae Min Lee had gone missing. In turn he asked whom I thought I told that information to and then about visiting the Syed family shortly thereafter. I was asked what prompted me to write to Syed in the first place and why I wrote 2:15-8 PM in parentheses in my first letter. I responded by saying that Adnan's family had indicated to me that he was having trouble recalling all of his actions on January 13th, 1999. I assumed that by writing to him perhaps I could jog his memory about the fifteen to twenty minutes of our library encounter. I also assumed that if he could remember that time period, perhaps it would lead to the memory of his other activities and possibly the recollection of other potential witnesses. Perhaps that could help him narrow the gap between the end of the school day until the time he visited his mosque (2:15-8 PM).

To me that explanation seemed like it should have explained my motivations, but for what I could only assume was for the clarity of the court, Brown asked if I could have been offering to provide Adnan with a false alibi. Of course I answered this with a resounding "No." Then came the part I most hated. Brown asked me to read aloud and explain the contents of my letters to Syed back in 1999. Normally reading aloud is not something that I disdain so much. In fact, I read Dr. Seuss aloud to my children quite often and I rather enjoy it. This however was very different. Reading aloud letters that you wrote when you were only seventeen years old is pretty embarrassing. I may as well have read my old diary entries. Worst yet was having to stop practically line by line in order to describe the intention and sentiment behind every phrase. Although a necessary evil, it felt like public torture. Ever since the letters have been made available on the Internet (thanks to Sarah and the SERIAL team—by the way, thanks) they have been the topic of much scrutiny and conversation. People from all over the world have not only read the letters but have expressed their own interpretations of their words. People have analyzed and argued over the most minute and asinine details, while all together forgetting that they are the work of a seventeen-year-old girl. Personally I'm insulted that I didn't get more flack over the clip-art. Nonetheless, I guess it was only a matter of time before I was asked to explain the letters myself. So there I was sitting before a crowd of strangers, trying to put myself back into the shoes of my seventeen-year-old self. Eventually that passed and Brown began to ask me more details about my interaction with Rabia Chaudry on March 25th, 2000. He wanted to know how I had come to write and sign the affidavit, and more specifically if I had felt pressured to do so. I of course responded by telling him my full account of the experience and stating that I was indeed not pressured to write or sign anything. All of my testimony up to this point was neither especially exciting to me, nor was it unexpected. Ever since I decided to come forward I was under the impression that I would eventually be asked these questions in a court of law.

What followed next was my favorite part of my testimony because it was my opportunity to give a full account of my phone conversation with Kevin Urick, a story that hardly anyone had yet to hear. The minute Brown started down the path of describing the pretenses of my phone call to Urick, I perked up.

I explained the situation of the private investigator reaching out to me through my husband. I described the methods in which I came to speak to Kevin Urick on the phone. I described the contents of my conversation with Urick and then provided the contemporaneous notes that I had taken during that conversation back in 2010 (mic drop). Mr. Brown then placed the notes on the projector screen for the entire courtroom to see and it was as if a silent gasp could be felt within the room. That was a good moment. In any case, I can't recall if it was an actual objection but Vignarajah stood up and addressed Judge Welch: "Excuse me, Judge, do we know if these exhibits are the originals or if they are copies of the original documents?" (He was talking about my hall pass and the Urick notes). I felt my face forcefully hide a scowl and an eye roll.

Before Brown could even respond I chimed in, "I actually brought the originals, your Honor. They're actually in my purse in the hallway with my husband." I knew what Vignarajah was trying to say and I knew exactly what he was about to attempt: he was going to argue that the documents could not be accepted because they were copies of the ones in my purse. The reason that they were copies is because I was apprehensive about giving up the originals. As I told the court that day, I keep everything. Well, not everything, I'm not a hoarder. I am, however, very smart and can be very premeditated at times when it comes to saving keepsakes. To me the notes and my hall pass are extensions of my memories. As I've discussed before, I don't like to let go of my memories. Nevertheless, I sent Gary out into the hallway to retrieve the originals and bitterly turned them over to the court, all the while knowing the chances of ever owning those documents again is slim to none. What followed next was more testimony about my call to prosecutor Kevin Urick. Brown asked if I was aware of the length of my conversation with Urick. I responded with something like, "thirty-four minutes." He then questioned how I knew this be true and I responded that my phone records had been retrieved from my wireless provider and that I had gone through every unknown phone number dialed on April 11th until I found the one in connection to Kevin Urick.

After that segment Brown began to get into more personal questions like why I chose to get a lawyer before re-involving my-self in this hearing. I told the court that it was because I wanted the truth to be heard and didn't want to be directly working with the defense or the prosecution. I don't think I mentioned this in court, but it was also because I wanted a layer of protection against misinformation and misguidance. Brown then asked if I had been subpoenaed to which I said, "Yes." Then he asked whether I would have participated in these proceedings without the issuance of a subpoena and I replied, "Yes." Then he asked me why that was the case, and I answered that the information within the SERIAL podcast had placed a great weight on my heart, and that I felt in order for justice to be achieved, that it

was my belief that all the viable information needed to be presented to the court. Simply put, that coming forward was the
right thing to do.

The Cross-examination

I believe that's when we took a short recess and then returned for
Vignarajah's cross-examination. As the cross-examination started the realization that I was officially in the hot seat dawned on
me. Not only were my words about to be examined with a fine-
toothed comb, but it was about to be done by the Deputy Attorney
General of the state of Maryland. If anyone could strong-arm me
into making a fool of myself, it would definitely be an attorney of
his caliber. After all, between the two of us, I was the only one
inexperienced with being in a courtroom. Thiru began his line of
questioning by asking how I was feeling. "Nervous," I replied. He
chuckled and made some kind of off-color remark in reference to
"being gentle" with me. Looking back, at the time I didn't think
much of it but now it kind of makes me shudder. I didn't realize
to what lengths he was getting ready to "bend me over" as they
say. I think that was his mild-mannered attempt to get me more
relaxed. Perhaps he thought that if I were at ease, I'd be more
likely to fall prey to his trickery. Either way, I wish I could say
that Thiru made me feel more at ease. I wish I could say that
what came next was effortless and as straight-forward as the
testimony that I shared with Justin Brown. Unfortunately, that
could not be further from the truth.

Vignarajah's line of questioning was not straight-forward in the slightest sense. It's my opinion that he made it a point to keep his questions as confusing as possible in an attempt to trick me into agreeing with him on certain points. In this strategy he failed. He made me feel as if I was dealing with a child who was trying to scam his way into getting the answers that he wanted. As if he were to ask me the same question enough times, in a different enough way, that my response would somehow be different. He obviously didn't take into account that I deal with that mentality every day. As a stay-at-home mother of two boys under five, I can say that Vignarajah's idiotic tactics over those two days is what annoyed and infuriated me the most. I thank God for the large bulldog paper clip that had been left on the witness podium. Pinching that clip became my saving grace because like a handheld stress reliever, it kept me calm.

During the first part of his cross-examination, Vignarajah asked me a series of questions that seemed to have both no purpose and no direction at all. He seemed to be obsessed with the fact that I had not gone to extreme measures to research details from the original trial. I was asked if I had ever obtained court transcripts, reports or various other items of evidence, all of which seemed silly to me. As I see it, my involvement in the case has never depended on what any other piece of information has to say about Adnan. My involvement in this case is a simple matter of quantum physics. Adnan's body as a whole is not capable of being in two places at one time. Based on our current technology it is physically impossible for Adnan to be both in the library speaking to me at the very same moment that the state argues that he was inside of Hae's car strangling her to death. I don't know if Vignarajah was trying to convince me otherwise or whether he was insinuating that my memory was false; in any case it was the first hint of his ongoing condescending tone.

I have to give Vignarajah credit, he worked overtime in his attempts to conceal the reasoning behind every question and he challenged me about every spoken and written word I've ever uttered in relation to this case. For example, he'd jump from situations that happened in 2015 to those that took place in 2000. He would then jump to things that transpired in say, 1999, and then fast-forward to 2010. Then, just when I thought I had cleared all his hurdles, he'd go back to the same question (rephrased) that he had asked me about hours before from the year 2000. It felt like he was asking me the same damn questions multiple times. In fact, I know he was because all the while Justin Brown was objecting:

"Objection, Your Honor, asked and answered!"

"Objection, Your Honor, she just answered that!"

"Objection, Your Honor, the witness already said that she doesn't remember!"

"Objection, Your Honor, does the court wish Mrs. McClain to speculate?!"

At one point, Judge Welch even suggested to Vignarajah that he speed up the nature of his inquiry and get to his point. Unfortunately, it seemed as if Judge Welch was in no mood to uphold any of Brown's objections. At the time it felt like a bad thing because with each over-ruling came a question that I had to answer again. However, looking back now I think Judge Welch did that strategically. I think he wanted the prosecutor to shoot out all his dirty arrows and let him employ all his efforts, so that in the end no matter Judge Welch's verdict, no one could say that Vignarajah didn't give his best efforts. No one could say that Vignarajah didn't work me over as best as possibly imagined. In any case, at the time, let's just say I was less than pleased by the merry-go-round approach to questioning that Vignarajah had for me. Gary thought Justin Brown's objections were hilarious because as he put it, I didn't need Brown. I was holding my own.

Over the next two days Thiru would continue to ask me silly questions like whether I enjoyed the SERIAL podcast and what my personal opinions were about Sarah Koenig as a journalist. How was it that I came to learn of Adnan's arrest? Who all did I tell I spoke to Adnan on January 13th? Did I tell Justin Adger about the January 13th encounter in person or over the phone? What was the location of that conversation and when was it that Justin and I decided to make arrangements to visit the Syed family? Who drove me to the Syed family home and did I know where they lived? Did I create a YouTube video when my attempts to obtain my Sprint phone records fell through? Just a whole bunch of questions that made me feel like he was trying to overload me with minor details that weren't necessarily important in terms of seeing Adnan, where I did, when I did on January 13th, 1999.

Vignarajah asked questions that alluded to me being privy to other people's private conversations, like if it would surprise me to know about Hae's friend's opinions about Syed's personality or their concerns over his demeanor. It felt as if Vignarajah was trying to influence my opinion of Adnan's guilt, and as if he were inconspicuously trying to make me into an "Adnan guilter" instead of an unbiased witness. At any rate, Vignarajah would then also ask me to speculate on other people's intentions and interpretations as if I were a telepathic mind reader. At one point he asked me why I thought Syed would go to the public library at the front of the school when the track was in the back of the school. To this I thought, *Really? How the hell should I know?* but instead I answered much more cordially: "Sometimes the track practice doesn't start at the track. Sometimes it starts at other locations on the school grounds." As if he didn't see the error in his line of questioning, Vignarajah then asked my opinion of why Syed allegedly changed his routine on January 13th and use the public library instead of the school's internal library. Without even thinking I blurted out "His prerogative?" and the courtroom erupted in laughter. I mean really? How in the hell am I supposed to know why a person chooses to do one thing one day and a different thing the next? As I said in court, sometimes people make random changes to their routines. Some things are just really, really bad coincidences. For all I know Adnan was hungry that day and decided to grab some food at the diner or 7-11 across the street. Perhaps he figured he'd kill two birds with one stone and check his email at the public library on his way back to track practice. Who knows?

Nonetheless, Thiru asked me more silly questions about my social life and social status. Did I tell many people about my encounter with Adnan back in 1999? At one point he implied that I had purposely kept the encounter as some sort of dirty little secret, but at another point he implied that I had used it as a means of seeking attention. He was literally all over the place with his accusations, throwing poop everywhere just to see what would stick and what he could get me to admit that I did not remember.

Thiru would grill me about the order of my class schedule from 1999. Did I write my second letter in CIP class and which period was that? Never mind the fact that in my second letter to Adnan it says that I was writing during CIP class and that I had to go because I had to attend third period (co-op). I thought it seemed pretty redundant for him to ask me a question that he already had the answer to. The best answer that I could provide was to refer to the contents of my letter(s), because to this day I can't even recall what CIP stood for. After all, how many of you over thirty-two years of age can remember the exact order of all your classes your senior year of high school. Hell, how many of you can remember what you ate for lunch last Tuesday?

Nevertheless, Thiru pressed on. Did I have CIP class before Spanish class or the other way around? What sports did I play my senior year? Did I play basketball; did I bowl? The questions were exhausting and seemed never-ending. I was ready for them to stop but Thiru just wouldn't let up. At one point I got so confused that I accidentally testified that I had played basketball my senior year. However, shortly after leaving the courtroom I started to feel very unsure of that information.

Throughout high school, I had only played a half of season of basketball because I had joined the team mid-season. The only reason I was allowed to do this was because both the players and the coach were all the same people from my volleyball team. After I got home from that first day of court, I quickly began to realize that my memory of that event included an upperclassman that graduated in 1998. I called a few friends to confirm my suspicion, and determined that it was impossible that I had played basketball my senior year. No harm, no foul though, because I simply volunteered a correction to the court and it wasn't a big deal.

At any rate, Thiru plugged on about my relationships in high school, in particular, whether one of my best friends, Stacie

Allen, was known in high school as "White Girl Stacey" (from my second letter). I laughed and said, "No, she's Black Girl Stacie." This once again caused laughter in the courtroom. Side note: my friends and I will forever call her that now. This consequently would be the moment I realized why Vignarajah had treated Stacie with so much disrespect the weekend prior to court. He thought she was a person of greater interest than she was.

Up until this point, none of Vignarajah's questions seemed even remotely relevant to the reason we all were there. Until he began to ask me about my conversation with Kevin Urick, the only effective thing that Vignarajah successfully achieved was getting me to say "I don't know" or "I don't remember" a lot. Even his questioning about my conversation with Kevin Urick seemed rather futile. Asking me whether Kevin Urick knew me to be an alibi witness for Adnan Syed (during our conversation in 2010) and whether Urick was aware of the existence of my 2000 affidavit seemed like a pretty foolish question to ask. I had just explained that when I called Urick, I introduced myself as a potential alibi witness for Syed. I can only assume that perhaps Vignarajah had forgotten that part of my testimony, the same way he had forgotten Urick's 2010 post-conviction testimony in which Urick stated:

"...She [Asia McClain] was concerned, because she was being asked questions about an affidavit she had written back at the time of the trial..."

Other than plain-old forgetfulness, what was the point of having Judge Welch or myself sit through that line of questioning? Did Vignarajah forget that Welch was the original post-conviction Judge?

In terms of information I failed to know or remember, most of it was information that seemed unremarkable and will probably be forever forgotten or unknown to my mind. I can't say that everything he asked was of little significance. Vignarajah may have scored a point with the whole affidavit issue with Rabia. During my cross-examination Vignarajah asked me if I would be surprised to know that Rabia had testified (in 2010) saying that she contacted me prior to showing up at my house. I said yes, it would surprise me—again, because I don't remember Rabia scheduling the encounter ahead of time. I do remember Rabia coming to my house and going to the notary. I don't remember anyone else being in the car and I remember her accidently driving past my house when she dropped me off. Although I am positive that my memory is accurate and it's Rabia's that is flawed, who's to say that the truth isn't a combination of both our memories? Perhaps she did call ahead to schedule a time but was late and I was surprised when she finally showed. Perhaps she did come to my house and we went to the library then the notary. Perhaps that's why I remember feeling so annoyed that she was taking up my afternoon. Perhaps Saad was in the car, but in the back seat. Perhaps I simply don't remember him being there. Perhaps when she dropped me off at home Rabia did embarrass herself by driving two doors past the very house that she had just left earlier. It's possible that both our accounts are correct. I think it's silly to assume that one of us has lied or committed perjury.

Vignarajah then asked if I would be surprised to know that Rabia had previously said that I attempted to call the police and attorneys along with the Syed family (in 1999). The minute he said this I instantly recognized it as a trick. I don't know why but I saw this statement as something that he had taken and twisted to sound different from what Rabia had actually intended. Still, I informed Thiru that I would be surprised to know that. I also asked whether if Rabia had been referring to the contents of my 1999 letters to Syed and not actual verbal admissions from me, because I knew for a fact that Thiru was referencing a non-existent conversation.

Soon after this Thiru attempted to exploit my memory of the weather on January 13th, 1999. Sadly, for him, he was unsuccessful because there was no specific memory to be had. He brought up the fact that it snowed the week prior to January 13th. He used that fact as an opportunity to question the accuracy of my memory. He reiterated what I'd said to Sarah Koenig about my memory being tied to the first snow of the year. I then confessed that my conversation with Sarah consisted of a poorly communicated guess. I admitted to the court that I don't remember the weather the night of January 13th. I just remember calling my mom and telling her that I needed more time to get home from Derrick's house because the weather was bad. My mom bought the excuse and Derrick and I were free to enjoy more time together. How long? I couldn't tell Vignarajah for sure. All I could do was continue to restate that I do know that school was closed the following two days and that fact made the night owl in me very appreciative. Vignarajah eventually abandoned that approach and began to take on some more offensive ones.

The first thing he attacked was the contents of my letters. He badgered me about how I came to know that the library had cameras (which is something I stated in my first letter). I told him that I had called the library and whoever answered the telephone confirmed that they had a video surveillance system. He responded by asking me to state when that call took place and of course that was a question that I could not answer.

Vignarajah then referenced that I had not put a specific alibi time in my first letter. He asked if I could see how someone could read my letter (the part about 2:15-8 PM) and think I was offering to cover more than fifteen to twenty minutes of Adnan's day (a false alibi)? To me the question was idiotic because at the time I wrote Adnan the letters I wasn't anticipating that anyone else would be reading Adnan's mail. When you think about it, if a third party was going to attempt to interpret my message intended solely for Adnan, then the fault of misinterpretation should fall solely on that person, not me. In truth, that person could make whatever assumptions their brain could muster. Hell, they could assume that Asia McClain wasn't even a real, live, breathing person, instead a figment of Adnan's imagination (AKA the next conspiracy theory to hit the web). I just can't see how my testimony or I should be held accountable for such an error, so that's basically how I addressed Thiru's question.

After that Thiru wanted to address the manner in which my second letter was written. Was it previously a hand-written letter that was later typed? Yes. Did I write it during CIP class and if so, where's the rough draft? Come on now! Really? Where's the rough draft? It's been over sixteen years! For all I know that letter has since decomposed in a landfill and been reincarnated as a noxious ground weed. Thiru didn't see it fit to stop there; he began to give me the third degree over why I joked about Adnan getting named prom king.

Then Vignarajah pointed out that in the heading of my second letter to Adnan, I had placed Adnan's inmate ID number. He pressed me on how I gained knowledge of that information so soon after his arrest. The hell if I know, so I admitted that I could not recall. He questioned how I knew about Hae's shallow grave and details including the location of her corpse. This question hit me the hardest out of all his questions. As I tried to answer I found myself thinking about Hae's dead body. The image of her lifeless foot sticking out from her shallow grave flashed in my mind. I was only able to get out two sentences when I simultaneously thought about my grandfather's best friend who had just died weeks before. I thought about the last time I had been to Baltimore and saw Mr. Dave. How he had just held my son and me in his arms and hugged us so hard that it hurt.

As I began to cry I choked up the words, "Whenever someone passes, you try to remember when you last saw or spoke to that person. When we found out that Hae was dead, I tried but I couldn't remember when I last saw Hae, but I did remember talking to Adnan about her on January 13th in the library." With that one statement, the tears came and I began to cry. Once the tears came, my face began to uncontrollably wince up. The thought of what happened to Hae all those years ago often makes me very sad. Add in pregnancy hormones and it took me a moment to get my tears to stop. Luckily, Vignarajah and Brown had just asked Judge Welch to approach the bench. What the two legal teams discussed with Judge Welch is beyond me. All I know is that someone gave me tissues and Vignarajah asked me if I needed extra time to get myself together. I refused, dried my eyes and continued to answer his questions.

As we went on, Vignarajah questioned my knowledge of terms like "central booking" and "fibers." Considering that I had already admitted to not knowing the technical term for where new inmates are held, he found it peculiar that I would use the term "central booking" in my letter. For this I had no particular explanation. Kids gossip. Who knows? Vignarajah insinuated that there was no possible way that I could be familiar with such terms outside of being spoon-fed them by Adnan himself. Vignarajah asked if anyone had put me up to writing to Adnan. I responded, "No." Then he accused me of writing my second letter on or after March 20th, 1999, and backdating it in order to serve as a false alibi. He highlighted things like my usage of phrases like "The other day (Monday)" and "the gossip is dead for your associates; it's starting to get old." I of course thought these accusations were complete nonsense. Frankly, it pissed me off and I wanted to tell him to leave me the hell alone. I can't even entertain a scenario in which I would be ballsy enough to involve myself in such a high-stakes, low probability-of-working scheme, let alone carrying it out for over sixteen years, when I could have easily have walked away, free from the risk of perjury back in 2010. The idea is as far-fetched as it is stupid. So I answered the question the most respectful way I could, by stating that what he was claiming was impossible because I did not write my second letter on or after March 20th; I wrote it on March 2nd and I left it at that.

Just when I thought his insults were done, Vignarajah came forward with the mother lode of conspiracy theories. He talked about a handwritten note by one of the Baltimore city detectives back in 1999. Apparently they had conducted an interview with a fellow classmate Ju'uan Gordon. At some point after Adnan's arrest, Ju'uan had been in contact with him. During one of these conversations Adnan mentioned something about wanting character reference letters in addition to letters that might assist him with bail review. Apparently during Ju'uan's police interview he told them about this interaction with Adnan. Ju'uan said that Adnan tried reaching out to other students for assistance with letters. In some manner Ju'uan mentioned that Adnan communicated the intention of asking me to send such a letter. Unfortunately the police officer's notes from this interview looked very vague. All that I see is a vague reference to my name and another note with my name listed with a question mark next to it. I think that's the reason Thiru didn't enter the police officer's note into evidence. I don't think he wanted Judge Welch to see how bullshit it was.

Personally, when I look at the notes I envision a scenario in which Ju'uan was confused. I could easily imagine him confusing the knowledge that I had written Adnan letters with Adnan asking for letters. I could see the possibility that Ju'uan may have been under the impression that I didn't think my first and second letters had ever reached Adnan. After all, I was never contacted by the defense and never understood why. If only I could remember whom I told about writing letters and whether I was under the impression that they had not been received. Then, I could say for sure that Ju'uan knew about it prior to his police interview and simply confused the two scenarios as being the same. Perhaps that is what resulted in the police notation "she got the address wrong."

In any case, during his cross-examination Vignarajah used this vague notation as a means of including me in some sort of outlandish conspiracy to provide Adnan Syed with a false alibi and character witness. He also tried to state that had I received such instructions from Adnan, it could have provided the foundation for my knowledge of certain key case facts (central booking, shallow grave, fibers, etc.) Feeling completely slandered I responded with the only thing I could say. Adnan, nor anyone from Adnan's legal team or family, had ever contacted me in regard to writing Adnan an alibi or character witness letters.

Vignarajah of course didn't accept this as truth, seeing that he continues to slander my character and lie about my motivations both in court and via any press conference awarded to him.

Redirection

After Vignarajah's attempts to discredit me were through, it became Brown's turn to redirect. Once again, Brown brought into question my 1999 library conversation with Syed. This time he inquired about specifics, mainly who brought up Hae in the conversation. "I did," I answered.

Then Brown attacked Thiru's cockamamie theory that I was a co-conspired and false alibi. Brown reiterated that fact that I had both written a rough draft and typed a finished version of my second letter to Syed (in 1999). He then asked if upon typing my letter I had taken the liberty of adding things that weren't included in the first letter. I confirmed this to be true and Brown continued. Brown stated that considering I had not typed my second letter until later on the day of March 2nd, I had approximately two days to gather intel and rumors from other students. I confirmed again and then Brown asked if I had been aware that police had interviewed several students in the days after Syed's arrest and in between mailing my second letter. "Yes," I answered.

Then Brown asked if there was a possibility that I may have interjected my new-found intel and rumors into the final draft of my second letter. "Yes, I definitely did!" I answered. With that, Brown questioned how I came to know certain details, like the fact that Syed was in central booking and the fact that Hae's body had been found in a shallow grave. However, he asked whether it was possible that information could have been part of the student rumor mill. I concurred that his theory was the more likely. As I did, I once again recalled hearing about Hae's murder and all the imagery that comes along with those memories. I felt the tears start to come again, but this time I was able to choke them back before embarrassing myself.

Then Brown did something that no one expected. He walked over to the projector and placed two *Baltimore Sun* clippings on the screen. One article was from February 12th and the other from March 1st of 1999. In the first article dated February 12th it reads:

"The body of a young woman found Tuesday **buried in a shallow grave** in Baltimore's **Leakin Park** was identified yesterday as an 18-year-old Woodlawn Senior High School student who disappeared nearly four weeks ago."

The second article read:

"Adnan Musud Syed was arrested about 6 a.m. at his home in the 7000 block of Johnnycake Road in Woodlawn, Baltimore County, and **taken to the Central Booking** and Intake Center, where he was charged as an adult with first-degree murder."

Then Brown looked me square in my face and asked if there was any possibility that anyone from school may have seen these articles, and whether it's safe to say that the information contained within the articles was common knowledge. "Yes," I answered, and in that moment Justin Brown became my hero.

Up until Vignarajah put the screws to me, I had never questioned how I came to know certain details. I simply didn't have an answer for how I came to know particular pieces of information sixteen years after the fact. Outside of gossip from other students who had been interviewed by the police, I never would have remembered whether or not the information had been in the press. I realize now that it should have been an obvious assumption on my part. Brown then followed up by asking if I had ever been asked by Adnan, his family or anyone else to write a letter providing an alibi. I answered no to this of course.

As part of his closing statement, Brown asked if anyone from the current prosecution had reached out to me in regard to the current hearing. I answered that my lawyer, Mr. Proctor, had indeed extended a personal invitation to Vignarajah soliciting my participation, but that no one from the state had contacted either of us, after which, Brown said something to the effect of: "Mrs. McClain, back in 1999 were you ever contacted by anyone on Syed's defense team?"

"Unfortunately, *no*," I answered. With that Brown was done.

Now, almost like a scorned revengeful little man-child, Vignarajah stood up to redirect with one abrasive question towards me.

"Isn't it true that the last time you talked to a prosecutor in this case, you went on to call him a liar?"

When Thiru asked this question my blood began to simmer just a little bit. Up to that point, I never engaged in name-calling any person of interest. I was so angry that Thiru would purposely accuse me of doing something that I had made a point to *avoid* doing. I looked him square in his eyes and with a smile and the glare of all the pissed off black women before me I said, "I actually never called him a liar. I've only ever stated what I know to be the truth."

This of course felt so good to say. As you can tell, I really don't care for people to who try to put words in my mouth. The fact that Urick misinterpreted and/or misrepresented the contents of our conversation doesn't make me the bad guy. The sentiment that how dare I challenge a prosecutor is one that I have had enough time to chew, swallow and digest. I'm absolutely 100 percent over it.

The Aftermath

After testifying I was asked to leave the room. Another witness was coming in to testify and because of the sequestration I was not allowed to hear their testimony. As I walked out of the courtroom doors, the only face I wanted to see was Phillip's. Only then could I begin to relax. I wasn't quite sure how I had done. I felt as if I had done well, however when you're addressing random questions in the manner I did, it can leave you feeling questionable.

As I hugged my husband, a slight sense of confusion came over me. Was Phillip up next? Could we leave? To our surprise we were told that Phillip's testimony was not going to be needed. Apparently, my testimony was found to have been so forthright and credible that there was no need to have Phillip corroborate a thing. I have to admit, hearing that news sure felt good. During the whole process I had felt so insecure about my testimony. It's amazing how the pressure of the scrutiny can make you begin to doubt yourself. You'd be amazed how easy it is to become obsessed with sounding truthful, regardless of the fact that you're actually telling the truth. I had to come to grips with the fact that my testimony wasn't going to be "perfect." Sounds silly to say, but from day one I have struggled greatly with the fact that I cannot remember more than I do. Even down to the moment when the words left my lips, I found it torturous to say the words "I don't remember" or "I don't know." It doesn't make matters any better when you have a prosecutor hell bent on making you say it as many times as he can. As if almost to use your own humanity against you.

Nevertheless, the more I said it, the more I admitted my own humanity, and the more I came to accept it. Like a mantra, it had reprogrammed me by the time Vignarajah was done. In order to endure, I had to be willing to accept the fact that I was not going to remember everything, that I was not going to say everything just right. In order to be of service to the truth, I had to be willing to put my reputation on the line. I had to submit to going under the process and hope that I would arrive at the other side unharmed. When push came to shove, I had survived the scrutiny of those who said I wouldn't show up to testify and those who said I would not stack up to the pressure of cross-examination. I had endured the combination of pregnancy hormones with the mixture of emotions associated with reliving all of these negative experiences over and over again. I had subjected myself to the intense eagle eye of not one, but two, seasoned attorneys, a judge and an audience of my peers. So when people emerged from the courtroom telling me that I had done well, that I was a rock star, it felt pretty damn awesome!

As Gary, my husband and I prepared to leave the courthouse, one of our new-found Sheriff friends asked if we would like to be escorted past the media. We took him up on his offer but to our pleasant surprise there were no cameramen outside of the courthouse. I don't know if they were inside watching the hearing or if someone had just screwed up. In any case, it was nice. Gary had notified me that morning that several media outlets had reached out to him requesting a statement from me after the hearing. I hadn't quite made my decision on whether I was going to participate with the media. The fact that there was none was a huge relief because the day before (and that morning), cameramen had bombarded us outside of the courthouse. Walking down the street with six cameras in my face is not something I am accustomed to. I didn't how to respond or where to look for that matter. I tried to pretend that the cameramen weren't there, but trying to see through six people as if they're translucent is just not possible. It's also very hard not to laugh when they trip, fall or walk into walls, because they are more focused on you than where they are walking. I had already been criticized for smiling the day before, so the morning of day two I decided to change my approach. In any case, it didn't take long for the media to realize they had missed their opportunity to get a statement from me. To be precise it only took literally ten minutes before Gary's phone began ringing non-stop. By that time, the three of us were already at Starbucks and I was in no mood to deal with the media.

Less than an hour after testifying, I found out that my baby might have Down syndrome. Phillip and I were still sitting in the downtown Starbucks when I received a message from my OBGYN. I gave them a return call to hear the scariest pregnancy news that I've ever experienced: the testing that I had the previous week had come back showing that the baby was at high risk for Down syndrome. I don't even remember exactly what the woman said to me, because I went into complete shock when I heard the words "Down syndrome." I don't know what she said the probability was, I don't recall what kind of tests she said I needed to have done, I don't even remember who she said was going to give me a call in order to schedule the additional testing. All I heard was... high rate... Down syndrome... testing... okay?

Meanwhile Phillip was sitting next to me trying to talk to me about something else. What it was I couldn't tell you either. In fact, while still on the phone with the woman from my OBGYN office, I blurted out, "Will you just shut up for a minute?" which of course is not the way I normally talk to my husband. When I hung up the phone I apologized but I was still in shock when Phillip asked me, "So who was that?"

I replied, "It was the doctor's office. They said the baby might have Down syndrome." It was at that moment that I literally could feel his heart drop to the ground where mine already lay. It was as if the time that followed stood still a few minutes.

Phillip then said, "Don't worry, babe, everything's going to be okay." Although I wanted to believe him, part of me just had this awful feeling that maybe, just maybe, everything wasn't going to be okay. I kept thinking to myself that maybe I did something wrong, but then my brain told me that Down syndrome has to do with chromosomes. I told myself that it was absurd to think that my actions had somehow contributed to this possible defect in my baby's development.

Then I started to feel guilty because I thought about the two miscarriages that we had the year before. I remembered reading an article about miscarriages, and that it said that most early first trimester miscarriages are a result of some type of genetic chromosomal or biological defect. That even though the cells are able to make a fetus, sometimes the fetus isn't viable and the mother's body rejects it. I thought to myself, *Maybe God knew something was wrong and that's why I had the two miscarriages. I kept thinking maybe God was trying to tell us to stop trying back then, and we didn't listen? Was that why this Down syndrome thing was happening to us?* Then I had the worst thought of all. *I'm not equipped for a child with Down syndrome. I'll have to literally take care of this person the rest of my life.* I even began to contemplate how cruel our society often is to people with disabilities. I became very pathetic in my thoughts. I began to sink into the center seat at my own personal little pity party. I started to wonder why was God doing this to us. I had just stood up and done something so great in the name of a Godly concept—truth. I began to feel as if God was testing me, yet again. I began to feel weary and tired of being tested. I got angry with God for bringing me this news. I couldn't believe his timing! Then I got angry at the idea that it seemed to be one thing after another after another. Nevertheless, my husband, the wonderful loving man that he is, could sense that I was hurting. He continued to tell me not to worry. "The baby is fine," he said. "Everything's going to be alright." And so I began to repress my feelings about the whole situation. Swallow the stress. Repress my anxiety in the hopes that I wouldn't think about it in that moment. Still, later that night the thought could not be pushed aside any longer and I brought it up to Phillip again.

Now let me back track a little bit in the day. When we arrived back from the courthouse I found my mother with the kids. She asked me how I was feeling and if I was okay. Being the discreet person that I am, I made a split second decision that I wasn't going to share the baby news right then and there. My husband, being the man that he is, immediately blurted out, "The doctor called and said the baby might have Down syndrome." Although I didn't show it I was very dissatisfied. I could not believe that he just blurted it out before we had a chance discuss if we were going to tell the family right away. I didn't express my frustrations at that moment, but later in the night when the conversation came up again I did.

During the conversation I told Phillip that I didn't know if I wanted to tell anybody else about the Down syndrome risk. That's when Philip looked at me very lovingly and in his most sincere voice said, "I do—I want as many prayers as we can get! I want as many people as we can get praying for this child." Being the Christian woman that I am and knowing the caliber of Christian woman that I would like to grow to be one day, I shook my head and agreed. It was then that I replied, "Well, if you want a lot of prayers, I might be able to make that happen," and giggled.

That's when the idea of sending a tweet came to mind. Initially it was not something that I took seriously—a joke at best. Then the more the thought lingered, the more it made perfect sense. I went to the Google App Store and I reinstalled Twitter. I logged in, erased a few old tweets that were really outdated and then chickened out! A few hours went by before I picked up my phone and opened the app again. So when I did, I decided to just start off slow and nonsensical. I sent a simple tweet to first notify those concerned about me in "Twitterland" that I was okay, exhausted, but still trying to keep my sense of humor about the whole situation. The tweet read:

"Talk about a crazy 2 days. It was really uncomfortable. Mentally & physically. That damn chair sucks! Poor hubby rode the bench literally :("

Then I began to look at the tweets of others and that's when I realized that as expected, my married last name was *everywhere*. I had always known going to court was going to force me to reveal my married name. It was an inescapable fact that I thought I had prepared myself for. All the same, seeing it all over the Internet was somewhat surreal. All this time, I had been given some sort of autonomy because everyone knew me as Asia McClain and not Asia Chapman. I had found peace in feeling like I had a little insulation from the social media crowd. Now I would no longer have that insulation. It was then that for the second time that week I told myself, "Screw it, deal with it, own it." So I tweeted:

"Wondering what the future holds next. #asiamcclain is now #asiachapman EVERYWHERE..."

Then I read a few more tweets and to my surprise everyone was unexpectedly obsessed with my red lipstick. I was flattered of course, so I thought to tell them where I got it (the same I had done with Thiru's associate). The thought also made me think of my good friend Tagen. After all, before I left Washington state, I asked her where she had purchased it and she replied by simply giving it to me. With the court ordered sequestration still in place, I wasn't able to discuss the hearing. Tweeting about lipstick didn't violate the sequestration and it just made sense for me to do so. Never did I once think that anyone would make it into something nefarious like some sort of marketing ploy. To me, it was a light-hearted and innocent tweet. It felt like a "Typical Asia" thing to say. Typical and normal is what I needed most.

Soon after I tried getting some rest, but I was still stressed. As a result, my sleep didn't last long and I woke up unable to fall back asleep. I found myself obsessively stressing over the baby and worrying about the whole Down syndrome possibility. My husband had fallen fast asleep and there I lay with him, but somehow I still felt alone. That's when I picked up my phone and tweeted:

"Can't sleep Got some worrisome news about the baby less than 1 hr after testifying #asiachapman needs prayers for baby. The more the better"

Almost immediately after I received a comforting reply, then a retweet, then another reply and so on. As I lay there in the dark, I suddenly didn't feel so alone. To my surprise people were receptive and cooperative with my request for prayers. People were friendly and hopeful. People made me feel supported and cared about. For the first time ever I really liked Twitter.

But, alas, there's always got to be at least one asshole in a crowd (right?). As I poured through prayer mentions and wishes of good vibes and hopes for my baby, my family and I, I saw a reply that made me mentally flip the bird. Some asshole that I will not give the benefit of mentioning, had written a horribly mean and morally barren tweet that I won't quote. I will simply say that it referenced my pregnancy struggles in relation to my testimony. Now I don't know why I didn't anticipate someone to stoop that low. We all have seen evidence of such atrociousness on social media before. I guess I just figured that my unborn child wasn't worthy of such idiotic debauchery. Apparently, I was wrong because there it was. So as quickly as I received that awful tweet, I blocked that waste of a brain, that incestuously spermed asshole from my Twitter account.

The most damaging thing about this case and SERIAL is being put on display for the whole world to scrutinize. It's not an easy thing to have every Joe Blow give his/her opinion about who they think I am. I thought I could read it all and take it in stride, but now I'm not too sure. Although I do laugh at most of it, there are those certain comments that bug me, mainly the ones that reference my appearance, personal choices, call me stupid, a pushover or call my actions or words nefarious. It's hard to keep close to your convictions while having other people drag your name through the mud. That's the primary reason this whole situation has been so stressful.

It's a weird thing to have people I have no personal attachment to discussing me in such a public manner, to be referred to as "A Great White Hope" and to be thanked by so many people from such a distance. One thing that I have been struggling with is having to distance myself from certain people simply because of their affiliations with this case.

Being positioned to feel as if I can't allow myself to be nice towards them feels so counterintuitive to me. It's hard because despite their bias on some matters, there are *some* instances when I can relate to a few of their sentiments and/or experiences. For example, one night I was watching a video where Rabia Chaudry talked about how Urick's Intercept interview made her feel. In the midst of viewing the video, I subsequently had to pause it in order to serve my children dinner. While doing so, I made a comment to my husband about how I felt about the interview. Ironically, upon resuming the video, I was tickled pink to hear that she had literally taken the words right out of my mouth. I couldn't help but laugh. My husband looked up at me and chuckled in amazement as well.

Another difficult emotion to stomach is the remorse I feel for both the Lee and Syed families. From the very beginning, I've always had a firm understanding of the grief facing both families. As a mother I can only imagine the pain they are bearing, both seeking for the lives of their children to be vindicated. Most of the crying I've done has been in the name of the Lee and Syed families. It really hurts to think that Hae's family is upset with me. I'm only telling the truth about what I know. Ask my husband—I had a total emotional meltdown when I read their statement that was released by Thiru after the post-conviction hearing in 2016. It definitely hurt me and I was devastated to the point where I cried about it for a long time. Most of the time

I feel like a piece of shit because I could be helping a murderer. Other times I feel like a piece of shit for calling Adnan a possible murderer. I'm damned if I do and damned if I don't. I try to find solace by not trying to determine Adnan's guilt or innocence. I try to stay focused on doing my part and letting the chips fall where they may. One thing I can tell you is that's a lot harder to do than you would ever imagine. I often find myself questioning why God allowed me to be stuck in the Woodlawn Public Library in the first place.

As troublesome as this experience has been, I have a hard time wishing that it all never happened. I try to remind myself that there is an important reason that God put me in that library on January 13th, 1999. I don't think the reason is as obvious as it seems, but I'm sure with time all will be revealed. Perhaps the point was as simple as to have me serve as Adnan's alibi? Maybe he truly is innocent? Perhaps it has nothing to do with Adnan at all? Maybe all of this has occurred to expose misconduct or problems within our criminal justice system. Perhaps this circumstance opens Hae's murder to new scrutiny and investigation. I had a conversation with one of my best friends and he stated his opinion on the matter. He said, "Guilty or not, perhaps Adnan may be serving a purpose outside of our own imaginations. We have yet to see what God has in store for Adnan nor are we privy to the knowledge of how many lives he has yet to bless.

It's possible that if Adnan is released that he could contribute something wonderful to his community, or help a multitude of people through community service or charities, etc. We just don't know. In addition, perhaps this experience has come to fruition in order for you to be that kind of blessing."

Either way, I cannot allow myself to close my heart to those possibilities. To say that I wish I had never spoken to Adnan or ever come forward would be to reject God's plan. I live by my faith in God's love and favoritism for his children. I can not ignore that God has used SERIAL to shed further light on this situation. Or that he saw fit to give me another chance to right my ignorance from back in 2010. I know from my own experiences that second chances don't happen all the time. I intend to make good on mine now that they have come around.

CHAPTER NINE

MY THOUGHTS

People of Interest

I don't know what people expect me to say about Hae, Adnan or Jay. I didn't really know any of them very well. I do have a couple of opinions, but not many. Most of what I feel for them is better measured in emotions and not words.

Hae

I didn't know Hae very well on a personal level, but I knew her in spirit. I knew her environment, her friends and her type of life. She seemed like a really nice person. I never heard her say a bad thing about anybody and I can't imagine her having any enemies. Whoever killed Hae murdered her in spite of her wonderful disposition.

I recently had a conversation with some of my best friends

and they informed me about a "Hae fact" that I had not remembered. Apparently Hae attended the same junior high school as I
did. Back then Hae was an ESOL (English as a second language)
student and was very meek and mild-mannered, so meek that I
don't remember her from those days at all. My friends tell me
that she was very quiet during those years and struggled with
her English. I can only imagine the determination and fortitude
it must have taken for her to become who she was at the time of
her death. She was a star athlete who dated a popular guy. She
was an excellent student with lots of friends. She was what all
immigrant parents want for their children. She was the American dream. I often think about how closely Hae's life resembled
my own. Her life was essentially the same as my life, her friends
very similar to mine. Her death could have been my death as
well.

It's a morbid thought to admit, but in my head I have
imagined Hae's corpse many times. It wasn't until recently that
I finally bucked up enough courage to actually read the autopsy
report. When I did, I found it extremely heartbreaking and eerie
to realize that my imagination wasn't too far off. After years of
relying on rumors, reading the report made things all too real.
In my head it's the closest I've ever come to the real evidence of
her death. I know that sounds strange because we all know that
Hae is dead. It's just to me, when people die, it's like they just
vanish. I don't know why I process death that way, I just do. To

read the report and know that someone really did those things to her just made me all the more angry that someone had stolen her life. I can't imagine any circumstance in which I would help someone do or even hide the evidence of something so awful. I can't imagine any scenario in which a person is ever normal again after participating in something so vile. Whoever took her life is a truly evil person. We may never know who that person is, but I believe that God knows. One day that person will have to face judgment for what they did and I would love to be there when they do.

Although this isn't really about Hae herself, I really dislike when people use the acronym HML in place of Hae Min Lee. I think if you are too lazy to type out her whole name, then just refer to her as Hae. For goodness sake, there aren't that many characters in her name. Show some respect! If you are going to talk about her death, the location of her death and who you think killed her, take the time to type her actual name. The acronym takes away from the fact that she was a real living breathing person. It takes away that she was a beautiful young girl. I find it so callus and cold to refer to her as HML. Enough said.

Jay

Let me start off by saying this. None of us know the true extent of Jay's involvement in Hae's murder, least of all myself. I can tell you that I never had a high opinion of Jay to start with. I never made fun of him, but I definitely didn't care much for him physically. To me he always seemed tall and awkward (gangly if you will). In my opinion he was often poorly dressed in what seemed to be the same type of outfit whenever we crossed paths. Stephanie, his girlfriend, on the other hand was gorgeous—one of the few girls at Woodlawn who made me feel a little self-conscious in the realm of good looks. She had gorgeous sandy blonde hair, bluish-green eyes and a pretty smile. I never did understand what exactly it was that she saw in Jay. To each their own, I guess.

As a matter of fact, upon recently looking through my senior book I was humored to see that under "weirdest couple" I had listed Stephanie McPherson and Jay Wilds. I'm not sure if I've ever even talked to Jay. I know I must have, but I just can't recall a specific conversation. The closest I can come to remembering any interaction with him is an event that took place possibly my ninth or tenth grade year. My volleyball teammates, other "jocks" and I decided we were going to goof off one day after school. We ended up getting into a random yet pretty fun game of tag. I say random because who plays tag in high school? We were generally way too cool for that, but that day we were having a wild hair and being goofballs.

If I recall correctly, I think Jay played tag with us. I think I remember laughing at him because he was cheating (go figure). He kept using his skateboard to get away! In any case, that day was all fun and games but as I said before, I never really cared for him much. I always saw him as a bit of a Dennis Rodman-ish kind of weirdo. I never had a desire to be friends with him because he was a self-proclaimed hipster before hipster was even a thing. He had a slacker type attitude with alternative music and lifestyle choices. When I listened to Jay's police interviews on the podcast, they struck me as odd for a number of reasons, the first being Jay's depiction of his high school reputation. In episode four of SERIAL Jay says:

"I'm the criminal element of Woodlawn...Perceived. It's like how the student body sees me. You know, I mean, people who really know me know that I'm not like that but, you know, you get a certain reputation and it kinda sticks with you."

Now again, let me say it, I didn't know Jay very well. However, I myself was pretty well known in high school. We didn't have many pretty girls named A.S.I.A. if you get my drift. Consequently, I am still friends with a rather large contingency of people from high school. That being the case, I've asked many people and have yet to find one single person who says that Jay was some sort of criminal badass in high school. Not one of us would even have considered him to have been the "criminal element of Woodlawn." Most people weren't even aware that Jay (says he) sold weed. If anything, most people that I have asked only remember that Jay was "odd," "a weirdo," "strange," "that he dressed badly," etc. A lot of my alumni remember that Jay often rode a skateboard, a few thought he had piercings and that he listened to a lot of heavy metal back then. None of which are deemed strange now, but back in the 90s it was very strange behavior for a black student at Woodlawn. Most people, myself included, say that they wanted nothing to do with him. So it's news to us that Jay was some sort of big time drug dealer. Is it possible? Sure. We all had connections to people who did bad things. We lived in Baltimore for God's sake!

All I'm saying is that if Jay was a drug dealer than he was the worst drug dealer ever! By his own admission he hung out with his clients and got high on his own supply, all the while still being broke. By his own admission he didn't have a cell phone or pager. He didn't even have his own vehicle. How on earth were people supposed to contact him about purchasing drugs? How did his clients get the product after ordering? Hell, by his own admission he and Adnan drove around on January 13th trying to find drugs. What kind of big time drug dealer is worried about being ratted out to the cops on a day when he has no drugs to begin with? What kind of big time drug dealer doesn't have friends that wouldn't beat the snot out of some dorky magnet kid trying to blackmail him? What kind of drug dealer doesn't understand concepts like probable cause or search warrant? What kind of big time drug dealer rats himself out to the cops? Doesn't make a lot of sense, now does it?

Another thing that doesn't make much sense is Jay's admission of having "murderous conversations" with Adnan. In one interview Jay can be heard telling the cops that Adnan bragged about murdering Hae. He says:

"...he couldn't believe he killed somebody with his bare hands, that all the other motherfuckers referring to hoods and thugs and stuff think they're hard core. But he just killed a person with his bare hands."

I've crowdsourced alumni opinions about this and by all accounts, it just does not seem like something that Adnan would say. In all actuality, in most people's opinions, it sounds like something Jay would have said.

Knowing what I know about Woodlawn, I don't think anybody questioned Adnan's "thugness." Adnan was a non-black, Baltimore County magnet kid from the Johnnycake area. He didn't have any "thugness" in him to question. The crowd of kids Adnan hung out with wasn't concerned with such matters and any "thugs" that he did have interactions with at school seemed to love him because of his generosity and kindheartedness.

In fact, I recently spoke with a guy that played football with Adnan back in high school. A picture of him and Adnan from 1998 recently surfaced on Twitter and became a topic of discussion. I talked to him about that picture and what he remembered from high school. He told me that there was no doubt in his mind that Adnan was 100 percent innocent. He said that Adnan is "literally the sweetest guy he has ever met in his life." He recalled times when he would be starving after school and

Adnan would share his own food with him. He accounted for a plethora of times when he would be stranded on the school campus after football practice and Adnan would take him home. The idea that Adnan would be concerned with the perception of his "thugness" just seems inconsistent with the accounts of his personality that I have heard.

On the flip side, in my opinion, the general perception of Jay's personality seems consistent with someone who might have said something like that. According to our alumni, Jay was a person who was constantly questioned about his loyalties. A lot of people questioned Jay's "blackness" and his "thugness" because of his attire choices, his personal interests and dating preferences. I am not saying that those words are Jay's words. What I *am* saying is that the resentful sentiment expressed within the confines of that statement (in my opinion) sounds more plausible coming from Jay rather than Adnan. I have asked many of my former classmates and we all agree, statements like "I'm going to kill that bitch" don't sound like something Adnan would say, certainly not in a serious connotation.

The other thing that disturbs me about Jay's police interviews is his admission of the knowledge of pre-meditated murder. In the very first episode of SERIAL Jay can be heard saying this:

"...During the conversation he stated that he was going to kill that bitch, referring to Hae Lee..."

At multiple times in several interviews Jay admits that he knew Adnan was going to kill Hae the morning of January 13th. If that is true, why, oh, why did he not tell somebody? If nothing else, why did he not at least warn Hae? In Jay's Intercept interview he appears to have admired Hae. Therefore, what bone did he have to pick with Hae that he deemed her life not worth saving? For me it's very hard to believe that someone who A) knew a murder was going to occur and did nothing to stop it would then B) have to be blackmailed into helping bury the deceased's body. Seems more logical to me that he possibly agreed to help dispose of the body (or more), before the actual crime was even committed. I know, personally, there's nothing that could have convinced me to help dispose of a dead body unless I was already involved in the actual murder. If I were a low-level marijuana dealer and an associate threatened to rat me out in exchange for cooperation, I would walk the other way. At that point I'd rather take my chances with the cops over drugs than a murder. Isn't it plausible to assume that Adnan would be way too busy trying to dispose of a dead body on his own to effectively get Jay in trouble for selling pot? In the same light, couldn't Jay have said something like, "Well, you tell the cops that I sell weed and I'm going to tell the cops that you have a dead girl in a car trunk?" Couldn't Jay just get rid of whatever small amount of weed he had at his grandmother's house and tell Adnan to kiss his ass? After all, the police never investigated Jay as a drug dealer, only as an accessory to murder. Also, Jay claims that he never touched Hae's corpse. If that's true, why did he feel the need to ditch his boots and clothes (according to Jenn)? Dirt can be washed away. Is it me? Am I the only one that doesn't understand the logic behind Jay's actions and participation in this crime?

The final thing that I will address is where Jay said Hae was murdered (and/or where he saw her dead body for the first time). Was it Best Buy or Edmonson Avenue? From what I have read online, Hae's cousin went to school at Campfield Early Learning Center (creepy...right around the corner from my grandparents' house). If that is true, then it takes approximately fifteen minutes to get from Woodlawn to the closest spot on Edmonson Avenue. It then would have taken Hae another twenty minutes to get from Edmonson Avenue to Campfield. It is possible for Hae to have done all of this driving and still be on time to pick her cousin up by three o'clock. However, not if there were any type of conversation with someone baked in. I could see Hae possibly stopping at the Best Buy, because it's right next to the highway that she might have used to get to Campfield. I don't see her driving out to Edmonson Avenue. Knowing the route that I normally took to get home, I think Best Buy is a little out of the way, considering that there is a huge, beautiful, secluded cemetery that connects the Woodlawn and Campfield neighborhoods (Woodlawn Cemetery).

Not only that—I have been to the Best Buy Jay says Hae was murdered at (and possibly saw her body for the first time?). It's not somewhere I would have gone to have sex with a guy. It's not somewhere I would have strangled a person (not that I ever would strangle someone). It's certainly *not* the place to transfer a dead body from the cab to the trunk of a car. It's not even remotely secluded. Out of curiosity I went to the Best Buy parking lot to see for myself. There is no crevice that is left unexposed to patron eyesight. No matter where you are parked, you can see the farthest parking spaces within plain view. Even the tiny asphalt portion in the rear of the store is located right in front of the store loading dock and the major roadway that lets you into the parking lot. It is just not plausible that Hae was murdered there. Not only that, there are cameras there. Were those cameras there in 1999?

Let's get one thing straight. I don't know if Adnan is guilty, but what I do know is that Jay is guilty of helping to dispose of someone's body. An innocent girl who was a friend to some of my very best friends. Hae was a sweet person with enormous promise. When she went missing, everyone knew about it and everyone said a prayer. She deserved so much better. I do think that Jay knows a lot more than he is willing to tell. Whether it involves more culpability on his part or perhaps other assailants is something only Jay can tell us. Since he isn't willing or able to tell us anything more, I guess we will never know. So for Jay's

known part in Hae's tragedy, it's safe to say that my classmates
and I will forever consider Jay a scumbag.

Adnan

Adnan is the hardest for me to talk about. With him I often find
myself at a loss for words. What do you say about the guy that
you may be helping out of prison after over a decade? About the
guy who may or may not be a cold-blooded murderer? I know
Hae's and Jay's role in all of this, however I am still quite clueless
about Adnan's. Every time I find myself going down one path of
emotions, I'm reminded of the alternative path. Having spent
over a decade wondering about his innocence, I have visited both
sides of popular opinions. I have bounced from #FreeAdnan to
#JusticeforHae many, many times and in the end I'm left ex-
hausted. All I can really say is that whatever the case may be,
I hope he has found peace with God. Whichever way this whole
thing goes, he's going to need it.

CHAPTER TEN

THE END?

I know that there will be those who will criticize me for writing this book. Those who will say I did all of this for money. To those people, I would like to say this: you're entitled to your opinion but you are wrong. Until you have walked a mile in my shoes, you can't comprehend how strenuous and, at times, heart-wrenching this situation has been for me. You have no idea how it feels to be tied to this awful tragedy by nothing more than your own conscience and admission.

Writing this book is one of the most emotionally draining tasks that I have ever embarked on. There were times when I wanted to quit and many times when I temporarily abandoned this project all together. If it had not been for the love and support of family members and close friends, I would have never had the courage to finish it. Publishing this book is not something that I have taken lightly and it has required a tremendous amount of thought and effort for me to complete. With all the speculation and misinformation out there, I just felt compelled to set the record straight concerning my involvement. I know there will be a lot of people who will judge this book before even reading it. There are a lot of those who will worry about this book damaging my credibility as a witness. I want you all know that the last thing I would want to do is muddy the waters of justice. This book consists of my story and I think that I should have a say in how it is told. This journey has been one of many dips and curves and the outcome to this day is not clear. I hope you have enjoyed getting a peek behind the curtain. A chance to get more back-story. There's a lot that went on in between news cycles, as I am sure there is more to come.

Judge Welch is a gentleman. He is both kind and generous. I find it hard to believe that a man who would lend his coat to a freezing stranger would not be passionate about seeking the truth. Hopefully my part in all of this is done. The likelihood of the prosecution or the defense asking me to reappear in court is very low. The defense has already established me as an alibi witness for a particular time period on January 13th, 1999. The prosecution now needs to make their case without the 2:36 "come get me call" that Jay previously testified to. I guess the real questions are now whether they can and whether they even want to try.

As I think back to the very beginning of all this, I can't help but wonder what impact my testimony would have made at Adnan's original trial. Would he have spent over sixteen years in prison? Would there have even been a trial? If not, how would that have impacted Hae's murder investigation? What impact would that have on Jay Wilds's confession and plea deal? I guess it's all kind of spilled milk at this point. How ill-fated it is that we will never know those answers. I suppose in a sad way, we should all be grateful for the popularization of such travesties. SERIAL and its contenders seem to be shining an awful amount of light on many of the great injustices of our time. In our country there is supposed to be equal justice for all under the Constitution. Unfortunately, the system is so broken that many prosecutors only care about winning and not whether a defendant is truly guilty or innocent. Ultimately, the question still remains. Did SERIAL give Adnan a do-over? So far, I'd definitely have to say yes, but to what extent? I guess we will just have to wait and see.

Since episode one of SERIAL, the infamy of this trial has grown beyond belief. It was only a matter of time before my face was plastered across the Baltimore six o'clock news. Now to some that might seem like a thrilling occurrence, but to me it has become a chore to tolerate. I might like to dress nice and talk/post about things other people might deem "domestic" or trivial, but at the end of the day I'm no "fame junkie." I am a stay-at-home mom and I enjoy my simple life—it isn't an episode of *Real Housewives* and it's certainly not reality TV-worthy in any sense (so don't hate). In the past, I didn't really anticipate that SERIAL would become so popular. I know for a fact that Sarah Koenig didn't either (no one did). I never anticipated that people would take such great interest in me, or that such great debates would be sparked as a result of my words and actions. I can't say that I'm flattered, because the spotlight is often quite blinding. These debates concern me more because they only highlight people's disconnection to other human beings. The nature of Internet's autonomy and the curiosity within human nature allows assholes to flourish. People are so quick to fully express themselves online these days, often with little or total disregard for those that they may be harming in the process. In my opinion, there is a certain level of freedom that our Internet community must begin to use more responsibly.

In closing, there is one major aspect of this whole circumstance that I have been struggling to wrap my head around. Like many of you, the unforeseeable end to all of these court proceedings appears very grim. Many of my classmates and I agree: every time it appears that things are headed towards the finale, there seems to be some sort of new development. With every progression comes something that ultimately is left to the mercy of a judge or jury. As a result, the whole process seems never-ending. I can only imagine what the Lee and Syed families must be feeling. Month after month, year after year passing not knowing what the future holds for Adnan. My classmates and I agree. No matter how long or hard this process is to get through, it is worth it if we can all someday find peace. Every step in this process, no matter how arduous, is important. Every step brings us closer to closure, no matter the end. As for myself, I take pride in the lessons I have learned throughout this process. I am solid in my belief that I have done the right thing and that my motivations have always been of the best intentions. I look forward to the day when we all can say that this situation is settled. Until then, all any of us can do is pray for the best and live life one day at a time. God Bless.

THE DOCUMENTS

LETTER #1

It's late.

I just came from your house an hour ago.

March 1, 1999

Dear Adnan (hope I sp. it right)

I know that you can't visiters, so I decided to write you a letter. I'm not sure if you remember talking to me in the library on Jan. 13th, but I remembered chatting with you. Throughout you're actions that day I have reason to believe in your innocense. I went to your family's house and discussed your "calm" manner towards them. I also called the Woodlawn Public Library and found that they have a survailance system inside the building. Depending on the amount of time you spend in the library that afternoon, it might help in your defence. I really would appreciate it if you would contact me between 1:00pm - 1pm or 8:45rpm until... My number is (410) 486-7655. More importantly I'm trying to reach your lawyer to schedule a possible meeting with the three of us. We aren't really close friends, but I want you to look into my eyes and tell me of your innocense. If I ever find otherwise I will hunt you down and wip your ass, ok friend. //

EXHIBIT
4

LETTER #1 Continued

I hope that you're not guilty and
~~e~~ I ~~west~~ hope to death that you have
nothing to do with it. If so I will
try my best to help you account
for some of your unwitnessed, unaccountable
lost time (2:15 - 8:00; Jan 13th)
The police have not been notified Yet
to my knowledge maybe it will give
your side of the story a particle
head start. I hope that you
appreciate this, seeing as though
I really would like to stay out
of this whole thing — Thank
Justin, the gave me a little
more faith in God, through his
friendship and faith. I'll pray
for you and that the "REAL TRUTH"
comes out in the end.   Only trying to help
"I hope it will set you free,"
                              Asis McClain
※ P.S. If necessary my grandparents
line number is 653-2957. Do not call
that line after 11:00   O.K.

Like I told Justin if your innocent
I do my best to help you.
But if you're not only God can help you.

If you were in the library for   Your Amiga
awhile tell the police and I'll
continue to tell what I know
even ~~kinder~~ than I am. My boyfriend and   Asia McClain
his best friend remember seeing you there too.

LETTER #2

Adnon Syed   #992005477
301 East Eager Street
Baltimore, MD. 21202

Dear Adnon,

How is everything? I know that we haven't been best friends in the past, however I believe in your innocence. I know that central booking is probably not the best place to make friends, so I'll attempt to be the best friend possible. I hope that nobody has attempted to harm you (not that they will). Just remember that if someone says something to you, that their just f**king with your emotions. I know that my first letter was probably a little harsh, but I just wanted you to know where I stode in this entire issue (on the centerline). I don't know you very well, however I didn't know Hae very well. The information that I know about you being in the library could helpful, unimportant or unhelpful to your case. I've been think a few things lately, that I wanted to ask you:

1. Why haven't you told anyone about talking to me in the library? Did you think it was unimportant, you didn't think that I would remember? Or did you just totally forget yourself?

2. How long did you stay in the library that day? Your family will probably try to obtain the library's surveillance tape.

3. Where exactly did you do and go that day? What is the <u>so-called evidence</u> that my statement is up against? And who are these WITNESSES?

Anyway, everything in school is somewhat the same. The ignorant (and some underclassmen) think that you're guilty, while others (mostly those that know you) think you're innocent. I talked to Emron today, he looked like crap. He's upset, most of your "CRUCHES" are. We love you, I guess that inside I know that you're innocent too. It's just that the so-called evidence looks very negative. However I'm positive that

EXHIBIT
5

March 2, 1999

LETTER #2 Continued

everything will work out in favor of the truth. The main thing that I'm worried about is that the real killers are probably somewhere laughing at the police and the news, that makes me sick!! I hope this letter and the ones that follow ease you days a little. I guess if I didn't believe in your innocence, that I wouldn't write to you . ☺

The other day (Monday) We (some of Mr. Parker's class) were talking about it and Mrs. Shab over-heard us; she said, "Don't you think the police have considered everything, they wouldn't just lock him up unless they had "REAL" evidence." We just looked at her, then continued our conversations. Mr. Parker seems un-opinionated, yet he seemed happy when I told him that I spoke to you family about the matter (I told him) Your brothers are nice, I don't think I met your mother, I think I met you dad; does he have a big gray beard. They gave me and Justin soda and cake. There was a whole bunch of people at you house, I didn't know who they were. I also didn't know that Muslims take their shoes off in the house…thank God they didn't make me take mine off, my stinky feet probably would have knocked everyone out cold.

 I over-heard Will and Anthony talking about you, they don't think you did "IT" either. I guess most people don't. Justin's mom is worried about you too. She gave me your home number, when Justin was in school. Classes are boring, that's one benefit to being "there", no school!!

They issued a school newsletter on the issue, so everyone is probably aware. It didn't say your name, but between that, gossip and the news, your name is known. I'm sorry this had to happen to you. Look at the bright side when you come back, won't nobody f**k with you and at least you'll know who your real friends and new friends should be. Also, you're the most popular guy in school. Shoot…you might get prom king.

You'll be happy to know that the gossip is dead for your associates, it's starting to get old. Your real friends are concentrated on you and your defense. I want you to know that I'm missing the instructions of Mrs. Ogle's CIP class, writing this letter.

March 2, 1999

LETTER #2 Continued

It's weird, since I realized that I saw you in the public library that day, you've been on my mind. The conversation that we had, has been on my mind. Everything was cool that day, maybe if I would have stayed with you or something this entire situation could have been avoided. Did you cut school that day? Someone told me that you cut school to play video games at someone's house. Is that what you told the police? This entire case puzzles me, you see I have an analytical mind. I want to be a criminal psychologist for the FBI one day. I don't understand how it took the police three weeks to find Hae's car, if it was found in the same park. I don't understand how you would even know about Leakin Park or how the police expect you to follow Hae in your car, kill her and take her car to Leakin Park, dig a grave and find you way back home. As well how come you don't have any markings on your body from Hae's struggle. I know that if I was her, I would have struggled. I guess that's where the

SO-CALLED witnesses. White girl Stacie just mentioned that she thinks you did it. Something about your fibers on Hae's body...something like that (evidence). I don't mean to make you upset talking about it...if I am. I just thought that maybe you should know. Anyway I have to go to third period. I'll write you again. Maybe tomorrow.

Hope this letter brightens your day... Your Friend,

Asia R. McClain

P.S: Your brother said that he going to tell you to maybe call me, it's not necessary, save the phone call for your family. You could attempt to write back though. So I can tell everyone how you're doing (and so I'll know too).

Asia R. McClain
6603 Marott Drive
Baltimore, MD 21207

Apparently a whole bunch of girl were crying for you at the jail...Big Playa Playa (ha ha ha he he he).

March 2, 1999

2000 AFFIDAVIT

Affidavit   a. R.M.

Asia McClain having been
duly sworn, do depose and state:

I am 18 years old. I
attend college at Catonsville
Community College of Baltimore
County. In January of 1999,
I attended high school at
Woodlawn Senior High. I
have known Adnan Syed
since my 9th grade freshmen
year (at high school). On 1/13/99,
I was waiting in the
Woodlawn Branch Public Library.
I was waiting for my ride from
my boyfriend (2:20), when I spotted
Mr. Syed and held a 15-20
minute conversation. We talked
about his girlfriend and he seemed
extremely calm and very caring
He explained to me that he just
wanted her to be happy. Soon
after my boyfriend (Derrick Banks)
and his best-friend (Gerrod Johnson)
came to pick me up. Spoke to Adnan (briefly)
and we left around 2:40.

EXHIBIT 2

2000 AFFIDAVIT Continued

A.R.M.

No attorney has ever contacted me about January 13, 1999 and the above information

Asia McClain 3/25/00

[illegible], notary

my commission expires [illegible]

URICK NOTES

No open cases

May 10 - 1st ten years of life sentence
case can be reopened if there is
new evidence.
Only within first 10 years of all
appeals exhausted; there is no
other recourse.

Brown is BS. Adnan lawyer not incompetent
despite health issues

No case ↑

Bunch of witnesses ready to testify that he was @ mosque backed down after cell records

Plea Bargain → Jay helped bury the body & testified

Cell phone records @ time came
Call from burial area of BODY

"If I had any doubt that Adnan didn't
kill Hae, it would be my moral obligation
to see that he didn't serve any time"

"Oh he killed that girl"
"There is snowballs chance in hell that they
could reopen the case with those accusations
let alone get him off"

2015 AFFIDAVIT

ASIA MCCLAIN

1. I swear to the following, to the best of my recollection, under penalty of perjury:
2. I am 33years old and competent to testify in a court of law.
3. I currently reside in Washington State.
4. I grew up in Baltimore County, MD, and attended high school at Woodlawn High School. I graduated in 1999 and attended college at Catonsville Community College.
5. While a senior at Woodlawn, I knew both Adnan Syed and Hae Min Lee. I was not particularly close friends with either.
6. On January 13, 1999, I got out of school early. At some point in the early afternoon, I went to Woodlawn Public Library, which was right next to the high school.
7. I was in the library when school let out around 2:15 p.m. I was waiting for my boyfriend, Derrick Banks, to pick me up. He was running late.
8. At around 2:30 p.m., I saw Adnan Syed enter the library. Syed and I had a conversation. We talked about his ex-girlfriend Hae Min Lee and he seemed extremely calm and caring. He explained that he wanted her to be happy and that he had no ill will towards her.
9. Eventually my boyfriend arrived to pick me up. He was with his best friend, Jerrod Johnson. We left the library around 2:40. Syed was still at the library when we left.
10. I remember that my boyfriend seemed jealous that I had been talking to Syed. I was angry at him for being extremely late.
11. The 13th of January 1999 was memorable because the following two school days were cancelled due to hazardous winter weather.
12. I did not think much of this interaction with Syed until he was later arrested and charged in the murder of Hae Min Lee.
13. Upon learning that he was charged with murder related to Lee's disappearance on the 13th, I promptly attempted to contact him.
14. I mailed him two letters to the Baltimore City Jail, one dated March 1, the other dated March 2. (See letters, attached). In these letters I reminded him that we had been in the library together after school. At the time when I wrote these letters, I did not know that the State theorized that the murder took place just before 2:36 pm on January 13, 1999.
15. I also made it clear in those letters that I wanted to speak to Syed's lawyer about what I remembered, and that I would have been willing to help his defense if necessary.
16. The content of both of those letters was true and accurate to the best of my recollection.

2015 AFFIDAVIT Continued

17. After sending those letters to Syed in early March, 1999, I never heard from anybody from the legal team representing Syed. Nobody ever contacted me to find out my story.

18. If someone had contacted me, I would have been willing to tell my story and testify at trial. My testimony would have been consistent with the letters described above, as well as the affidavit I would later provide. *See below.*

19. After Syed was convicted at trial, I was contacted by a friend of the Syed family named Rabia Chaudry.

20. I told my story to Chaudry on March 25, 2000, and wrote out an affidavit, which we had notarized. (Affidavit attached).

21. The affidavit was entirely accurate to the best of my recollection and I gave it by my own free will. I was not pressured into writing it.

22. At the time when I wrote the affidavit I did not know that the State had argued at trial that the murder took place just before 2:36 pm on January 13, 1999.

23. After writing the affidavit and giving it to Chaudry, I did not think much about the Syed case, although I was aware he had been convicted and he was in prison.

24. Eventually I left Maryland and moved to North Carolina and then out west.

25. In the late spring of 2010, I learned that members of the Syed defense team were attempting to contact me. I was initially caught off guard by this and I did not talk to them.

26. After encountering the Syed defense team, I began to have many case questions that I did not want to ask the Syed defense team. After not knowing who else to contact, I made telephone contact with one of the State prosecutors from the case, Kevin Urick.

27. I had a telephone conversation with Urick in which I asked him why I was being contacted and what was going on in the case.

28. He told me there was no merit to any claims that Syed did not get a fair trial. Urick discussed the evidence of the case in a manner that seemed designed to get me to think Syed was guilty and that I should not bother participating in the case, by telling what I knew about January 13, 1999. Urick convinced me into believing that I should not participate in any ongoing proceedings. Based on my conversation with Kevin Urick, the comments made by him and what he conveyed to me during that conversation, I determined that I wished to have no further involvement with the Syed defense team, at that time.

29. Urick and I discussed the affidavit that I had previously provided to Chaudry. I wanted to know why I was being contacted if they already had the affidavit on file and what the ramifications of that document were. I never told Urick that I recanted my story or affidavit about January 13, 1999. In, addition I did not write the March 1999 letters or the affidavit because of pressure from Syed's family. I did not write them to please Syed's family or to get them off my back. What actually happened is that I wrote the affidavit because I wanted to provide the truth about what I remembered. My only goal has always been, to provide the truth about what I remembered.

2015 AFFIDAVIT Continued

30. I took, and retained, contemporaneous notations of the telephone conversation with Urick.
31. Sometime in January of 2014, I had a conversation with Sarah Koenig, a reporter for National Public Radio. I spoke to her on the phone and she recorded the conversation. It was an impromptu conversation and I misunderstood her reasons for the interview and did not expect it to be broadcasted to so many people. While Ms. Koenig did not misrepresent herself or the purpose of the conversation and interview, it is fair to say that I misconstrued that it was a formal interview that would be played on the Serial Podcast. I rather thought that it was a meticulous means of information gathering, for a future (typed) online news article. Due to dialogue with Jerrod Johnson in 2011 concerning Derrick Banks, I recommended that Sarah Koenig reach out to both Jerrod Johnson and Derrick Banks, to see if they remember January 13, 1999. Later on, when Sarah Koenig asked to re-record my statement in a professional sound studio, I became confused and unwilling to participate in any further interview activity. As a result my interview with Sarah Koenig was incomplete in the Serial Podcast.
32. After I learned about the podcast, I learned more about Koenig's reporting, and more about the Syed case. I was shocked by the testimony of Kevin Urick and the podcast itself; however I came to understand my importance to the case. I realized I needed to step forward and make my story known to the court system.
33. I contacted Syed's lawyer, Justin Brown, on December 15, 2014, and told him my story. I told him I would be willing to provide this affidavit.
34. I am also willing to appear in court in Maryland to testify, if subpoenaed.
35. I am now married, and my legal surname is no longer McClain. However, due to the wealth of publicity that this case has had, and the fact that all previous mention of my name has been with my maiden name, I am signing below as Asia McClain.
36. I have retained counsel in Baltimore, Gary Proctor, and I respectfully ask that any attempts to contact me be made through him.
37. I have reviewed this affidavit with my attorney before providing it to Syed's attorney, Justin Brown.

_____

ASIA McCLAIN

DATE

Hae and Adnan at Prom

SPECIAL THANKS

I've learned the hard way that in my situation, you have to be careful. Anything that you say can truly be used against you in the court of law. Along the way, I have made mistakes, but I have never testified to anything that I didn't believe to be the truth. During this process I have had to learn a lot, especially not to openly speculate because people might see speculations as bias or untruth. Sounds like a weird thing to say, but being an alibi in a high profile case like this is stressful in this way. It makes you feel isolated because you don't have many people that you can trust. All I can say is thank God for the few people in my personal life that have been there for me and thank God for one cool-ass attorney. I'd like to take this opportunity to give a special thanks to these people. I love you.

Phillip Chapman

Michele Harrison

Alice Chapman

Tagen Kirk

Pastor Robert Bryceson

Anthony Morgan

Stacie Allen

Special thanks to people who have volunteered their time and patience to me. You guys have been my "gladiators."

Gary Proctor

Ali Pearson

Anastasia Karson

Jennifer Cohen

Robert Buschel

Danielle Castilla

www.mizecreative.com

Joshua Dahlstrom

Special thanks to everyone on the Internet who has shown me both respect and love. THANK YOU!

ABOUT THE AUTHOR

Asia McClain Chapman was born on June 26th, 1981, in Inglewood, California. Her parents, Carl and Michelle McClain, were separated in 1986 resulting in her relocation to Baltimore, Maryland. After growing up in the Baltimore County school system, Asia graduated from Woodlawn Senior High School in 1999 and proceeded thereon to college. In search of a fresh start Asia made the decision to drive across the country in 2005, toting nothing more than a Nissan 240SX and a U-Haul trailer full of her own belongings. After several years of living in Portland, Oregon, and working full-time as a personal assistant, Asia met her now-husband Phillip Chapman in 2008. The couple legally married in 2009 and they are now the proud parents of two rambunctious little boys, Lucas and Alexander Chapman. Asia is currently pregnant with her third child due in July 2016. Located in Spokane, Washington, Asia spends her days as a stay-at-home mother, board secretary of Solutions Automation and small business owner of Diamond Concepts. In her spare time, Asia enjoys writing, cooking, gardening and working with her hands in addition to editing her local MOMS Club International newsletter.